THE LOST GARDENER

THOMAS W. SANDERS
1855-1926
MARTLEY, WORCESTERSHIRE

by

David L.Cropp

THE LOST GARDENER

*

Published by Dave Cropp Books
2, Vernon Close
Martley, Worcs.WR6 6QX

*

First published 2001

*

*

ISBN: 0-9540178-1-1

*

Times New Roman 12

*

Printed and bound
by:
Cromwell Press Ltd
Aintree Avenue
White Horse Business Park
Trowbridge
Wilts.BA14 0XB

“Sanders played a very important role in the development of late 19th.century, early 20th. century gardening, and this has never been adequately recognised”

Arthur Hellyer, October 5th.,1990
Letter to Alan Boon, Martley

This Book is dedicated to Alan for his own dedication to the memory of T.W.Sanders

ACKNOWLEDGMENTS

I am so grateful to so many people for all the help and encouragement they have given me, first and especially Alan Boon who rediscovered T.W.Sanders and recognised his importance.

I would like to thank Jack Bradley, Brian Draper, Harry King, John Nicklin, Reg Snow, and Tina Steele - all Martley friends and true - for their individual support on the "Sanders quest" for his books.

I wish to record my thanks to "Amateur Gardening" for the loan of Sanders' desk for the Exhibition at Martley Summer Show in 1999, and Don Taylor, of Taylors of Martley plc, for the loan of the transport to help bring it home!

Other people in their own way deserve thanks. These include Yvonne Luke, of 'Herbaceous Books' Ilkley, for her help in tracking down a regular supply of lost books; Brian Simkins, of Spink & Son Ltd., of St.James' London, for his patience and perseverance in tracking down a Knight First Class of the Royal Order of Vasa Sweden, which King Oscar bestowed on Sanders in 1906; and Nancy Fagin, of Chicago USA, for the weighty task of arranging the return of six heavy volumes of "Profitable Farm and Garden" by air back to Martley.

I also wish to acknowledge Lewisham Local Studies and Archives Centre for the reproductions of "The Firs", by W.Mead; and Worcester Evening News, for permission to reproduce the rear cover photograph, and for their early support for this work.

David L.Cropp

CONTENTS

ILLUSTRATIONS

Page

- Colour Section -

** by courtesy of Lewisham Local Studies and Archives Centre*
*** by courtesy of Worcester Evening News*

INTRODUCTION: DESPERATELY SEEKING SANDERS

If you have already heard of Thomas Sanders , then I am very lucky, and so will you be! This is a story about trying to follow the last traces of someone who has long gone from the garden scene. It is as if someone has walked through, and left very little behind them.

Looking for T.W.Sanders has been a bit like that. Everywhere you can find the "footprints" of his life and where he has been, but so much of his story, especially some of the most important events, are still hidden away. So in a nutshell this is what I can tell you straight away.

Here was a local boy made good. He was born in the village where I live - Martley, Worcestershire. He came from a poor and relatively impoverished family, went to the local school for the usual length of time in the 1860's until he could earn his way in life.

Does he drift off into obscurity? No, seven years later he turns up as a gardening apprentice in The Palace of Versailles. Is that the end of his career? No, he goes on to become a renowned gardener, author, and editor for forty years from 1887 to 1926.

So, with such a pedigree, surely he must be well-represented in the history of late nineteenth and early twentieth century gardening. No, he is missing, with only one short mention of him, and that is of his death, in one gardening index.

Well, with nearly forty written by him, and another thirty edited by him, secondhand bookshops must be loaded with the books he wrote. No such luck! Apart from "An Encyclopaedia of Gardening" in its last editions, he is a very elusive writer and not easy to find on the shelves.

Web searching The British Library - such is the experience of modern technology! - you can find him well represented, with nearly eighty copies available, as well as all the journals he edited.

So at least he has some kind of existence, even if it is restricted to the stacks of our national library.

But where is the rest of the story which really tells us what spark of intellect, courage and creativity drove him from the poverty and obscurity of a rural cottage to the richness he finally achieved?

As far as I know, he has never been accorded his true position in the history of modern horticulture. Arthur Hellyer, a later editor of "Amateur Gardening" knew that :

> "T.W.Sanders played a very important
> role in the development of ..gardening, and
> this has never been adequately recognised."

We know from the obituaries in newspapers and journals that he had been a major and much-loved figure in the world of gardening for nearly half a century. He had a common humanity, and an eternal love for the natural world around him in cottage garden or countryside.

To the best of my knowledge, his story has never been told before, or if it has then I have failed to find it, and the fault is mine.

In some small way, and building on the outline of his life which Alan Boon kept going for him in Martley, I want to try to put the record straight in this book. I don't claim that this is a definitive work. I freely admit that there are some frustrating and yawning gaps, particularly when he was a young man and apprentice gardener.

I know too that I have not discovered all the articles he wrote for gardening magazines. Much of his life's work is still an undiscovered country for me. I just hope that through this book perhaps there is also a last opportunity for T.W.Sanders to speak to us directly from one century to the next.

T.W.SANDERS:
THE ROOTS
OF
A GARDENER
1855-1884

Thomas William Sanders was born on November 6th., 1855, in Martley, Worcestershire, and he was baptised at St. Peter's Church on December 9th. To tell the truth his family were most definitely poor. They had scratched out a living as labourers of one kind or another for generations.

But what do we know about his ancestors? His grandfather was also called Thomas Sanders, and we think he was born round about 1775, according to later census records. He had at least three sons - George, Thomas, and John (who was our Thomas's father). John was probably born in the Autumn of 1818. He is described variously as a bricklayer, a stonemason, and a labourer.

John Sanders married Mary Anne Callow on February 14th., 1853 - St. Valentine's Day, and no coincidence, because she was already three months pregnant with their first child. They were married at St. Martin's Church in Worcester. He was 34 and she was 27. They had an address in Silver Street. Worcester where I expect Mary was in service.

Mary's family came from the village of Suckley, Worcester. At her own baptism on September 24th., 1825, her father, William Callow was put down as an agricultural labourer. One of the witnesses at her marriage was James Callow who may have been her brother. The other witness was Hannah Severn, and she seems to have come from a family just as poor as the Sanders and the Callows. Later Workhouse records list a woman and illegitimate child going by the name of Severn.

None of them could write their own name. They were all illiterate, and all of them "made their mark" on the marriage certificate instead of a signature.

John and Mary set up home in a labourer's cottage at Quarry Farm, somewhere between Pudford Lane and Penny Hill, at Martley Hillside. Now the cottage is long gone. Alan Boon and I have found it very difficult to pinpoint precisely where it was, mainly because the official drawing up the census did not record in which order he listed the properties in that area. Frustrating!

THE FAMILY TREE OF THOMAS WILLIAM SANDERS

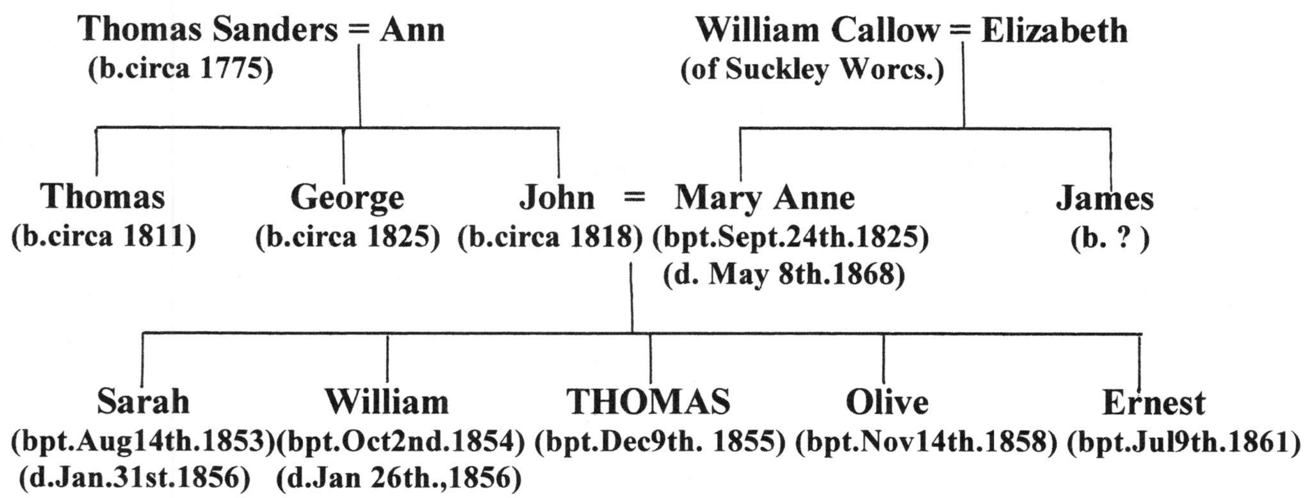

"VIEW" MARTLEY.

Wherever their cottage was, it was here that their first child, Sarah was born, and baptised on August 14th., 1853. Their first son William was baptised just over a year later on October 2nd., 1854, given the name of his maternal grandfather William Callow. Then one year later Thomas himself was born on November 6th., 1855 and baptised on December 9th. In the same tradition he was given the first name of his paternal grandfather Thomas and also his uncle.

Within two months tragedy struck the family. First, William was buried on January 26th., 1856, and then Sarah on January 31st. They were only sixteen and twenty months old.

We know that infant mortality rates were significantly high in the nineteenth century. Regular epidemics and childhood diseases were common. Poor nutrition, primitive sanitation, and inadequate hygiene and medical care did not help either. Death reaped a grim toll from the poor of both urban and rural communities.

The two savage blows that fate dealt the Sanders family that week can only be imagined. Afterwards, Thomas gained the second name of William, presumably to perpetuate the memory of his brother - the much-loved first son of John and Mary - and to carry on the link with Mary's father William Callow.

In time, Thomas William was joined in the family by a new sister, Olive, baptised on November 4th., 1858, and by a new brother, Ernest, baptised on July 9th., 1861.

We know that eventually their new first son was not going to disappoint them , though I suspect they had no idea in their little cottage on the hillside when they sent him off down the lane and the footpath across the fields for his first taste of education at the Village School.

Exactly what happened there I do not know. Thomas Sanders has given me one or two hints from editorials in "Amateur Gardening" that this is where his career as a gardener, editor, and writer really began. So this is where we turn to next - Martley Village School.

THE SCHOOL
MARTLEY.

According to the records, Thomas William Sanders was admitted into the Boys' Class of Martley Village School in February 1862 when he was just over six years old. Before that he may well have been in the Infants'Class at five. To get to school he would have taken a path across the fields and down the lanes from his Hillside home, finally arriving at the end of the path opposite the school gates between the two houses now called The Ivy and The Chandlery.

Free education for all the children of Martley had started on Tuesday, March 24th.,1846 when Dowager Lady Ward had officially laid the first stone of the new school, in the presence of the local gentry and landowners. Dowager Queen Adelaide had been one of the notable contributors to the fund for the school. When it opened William Henry Pennington was the first Headteacher, transferring from his post as a master at the Grammar School in Worcester.

It looks like Thomas's first experience of education was not entirely happy:

> "The schoolmaster was a tyrant of the Squeers type. So brutal was he that boys played truant, and there was little education."

But soon after, this teacher left, and

> "A new master came and a better era dawned."
>
> Amateur Gardening, October 23rd.,1926

Thomas's teacher would have been Michael Coleman, a man with his own reputation as a liberal educator. With him Thomas would have received a sound fundamental and traditional education for a country boy.

It was at school that he began to discover his real talent as a gardener:

> "We owe, in a large measure, our own love of, and interest in, gardening to lessons given after school hours by our teacher. He was passionately fond of his garden,

ADMISSION.

NAME.	Index number.	DATE.	Age. Y	Age. M	RESIDENCE.	Parent's occupation	M
Joiner Frederic	176	61·7	7	0	Hill-side	Labourer	
Adams John	177	61·7	5	0	Collings Green	Woodman	
Coldrick Thomas	178	61·7	7	0	Martley	Labourer	
Boucher William	179	61·10	7	0	Hill-side	Carpenter	
Hearne James	180	61·11	12	0	Doddenham	Brickmaker	
Lane James	181	62·1	13	0	Doddenham	Labourer	
Harris Arthur	182	62·1	7	0	Collings Green	Labourer	
Sanders Thomas	183	62·2	6	0	Near Brierly Farm	Mason	
Hodges Edward	184	62·4	7	0	Rummer's Farm	Bailiff	
Cottrill Alfred	185	62·4	19	0	Broadwas	Labourer	
Spilsbury George	186	62·5	9	0	Wichenford	Labourer	
Harding Thomas	187	62·5	7	0	High-fields	Gardener	
Kitson Walter	188	62·5	6	0	Hill Side	Labourer	
Freeman Joseph	189	62·6	7	0	Martley Mrs Morga	Servant	
Eaton Thomas	190	62·6	6	0	Hill-side	Labourer	
Holliday Thomas	191	62·7	12	0	Doddenham	Gardener	
Gwynne Thomas	192	62·10	6	0	Martley	Pig-butcher	
George Payne	193	62·11	11	0	Doddenham	Roadman	
Spilsbury Joseph	194	62·12	7	0	Wichenford	Labourer	
Crump Neighbour	195	63·1	13	0	Kenswick	Farmer	
Birch James	196	63·1	10	0	Doddenham	Shoemaker	
Grantham James	197	63·1	11	0	Doddenham	[illegible]	

and invited any boys who cared to spend an hour with him in the garden to do so."

Amateur Gardening, August 8th.,1903

Later he describes how he began to cultivate his own small garden area:

"Well do I remember trundling a barrow occasionally to school to enable me to gather manure from the roads to enrich my little plot, and home again to convey the produce I had grown with pardonable pride. It was this little plot of ground that first created within me a passion for gardening, and to it alone I owe my present position.

I look back upon those happy school days with much pride and pleasure, when I used to grow and know only by their common names the Monkshood, Jacob's Ladder, Indian Pink, Fair Maids of France, etc. - good old-fashioned flowers that are still held in high esteem as they deserve to be."

Amateur Gardening, January 18th.,1890

If he had an instinctive interest in horticulture then there were two large properties on either side of the school - The Old Rectory and Martley Court. Nearby there were other properties - The Noak, Laugherne House, and Barbers. Any of them could easily have provided him with the first chance to be an odd-job gardener. However he started, an owner or head gardener had enough intellectual ability, commitment, and interest in gardening to pass on their knowledge to Thomas.

School records show that pupils were often absent to help with seasonal tasks on their family farms and smallholdings. In 1863 (when Thomas was eight years old), absences were recorded for: setting beans and potatoes; treading wheat; picking cowslips; tending sheep; minding bees; collecting tree

"THE RECTORY COTTAGE"
MARTLEY.

bark; picking up cider apples; collecting peas and acorns for pig-feed; sowing wheat; wheat tying and binding; and turnip topping!

But in his own final years of schooling Thomas gave over some of his time to industrious and unpaid labour in his mother's cottage garden at home on the Hillside:

> "Happy memories still linger in my mind of my ancestral home on a Worcestershire upland, where, as a boy, I watched my mother gently tending the plants that flourished in her simple flower garden attached to the old Tudor house.
>
> I can see in the long vista of memory the old stone wall that divided the forecourt from the garden laden with yellow and dark wallflowers, filling the vernal air with their fragrance, the masses of sedum and stonecrop, pinks, and other old plants that flourished in the crevices and draped the wall with masses of greenery, and in due course, bright patches of colour.
>
> I can recall the monthly and the cabbage roses, the bush of sweet briar, the fragrant rosemary, the tufts of hyssop, rue, sage, and marjoram, that mingled with the lilies, double daisies, snapdragons, cloves, and auriculas, which use to make so pleasing an assemblage of sweetness, beauty, and usefulness in the old "flower knot" of those early days.
>
> No geometrical beds were required to grow these flowers, and no attempt was made to plant the flowers in regular lines or order. They were merely put in the simple borders, and the delightful ununiformity, coupled with their fragrance and the medley of colour, made that flower garden a source of real pleasure, interest, and beauty through all season."
>
> Amateur Gardening, August 29th.,1903

His mother died when he was quite young - he was only just

7128 B ROTARY PHOTO, E.C. THE ROYAL GATHERING AT WINDSOR, NOVEMBER 17th, 1907. W. & D. DOWNEY, LONDON, S.W. COPYRIGHT

KING OF SPAIN. EMPEROR OF GERMANY. QUEEN ALEXANDRA KING EDWARD

QUEEN OF NORWAY. EMPRESS OF GERMANY. QUEEN OF PORTUGAL. QUEEN OF SPAIN thirteen - and he devoted all his spare time to keeping his mother's flower beds beautiful.

He was no saint though:

> "One of his boyhood recollections was of King Edward (then Prince of Wales) and the ex-Kaiser's father shooting at Witley Court (Worcestershire). King Edward brought down a pheasant, and young Sanders, who was among the beaters, retrieved it. Another lad disputed his right, and a fight resulted.
>
> King Edward ordered a ring to be made round the disputants, and when young Sanders had settled the dispute by blackening the other boy's eye, King Edward smacked him on the back, and said: "Quite right; good boy," and gave him half-a-crown."

This was probably close to his time to leave school. There was now real poverty at home and there was the need for him to start earning. We know that:

> "When he was twelve his father decided he must be trained in the family business, and apprenticed him to a builder, but he hated it and wanted to become a gardener."

Yet even this turned out to be at first a blessing in disguise:

> "Curiously enough, his work as a builder's apprentice consisted of repairs to great hot-houses, and what he saw of magnificent exotic flowers and fruit with his love of gardening inherited from his mother, gave him a burning desire to become a great gardener.
>
> He ran away from home, and was found by his father in Worcester. and was taken back to his work. Still his idea persisted, and when he ran away a second time, his father let him please himself."
>
> Amateur Gardening, October 23rd.,1926

What happened next set him on the road to his future career:

> "Sanders succeeded in persuading an old gardener to have him as a gardener's boy at a very tiny wage, and the old gardener took to him, and taught him the rudiments of his craft."

The route forward as a trainee is no longer clearly recorded. We know that:

> "His sure instinct in many gardening matters was really due to the fact that his knowledge was founded on deep and wide experience - an experience that began when, out of his salary of 12s. a week, he paid 2s. a week to the head gardener for the privilege of working under him!"
>
> "From there he worked in various large gardens in Great Britain, also at Versailles, and in famous nurseries, until in 1884 he took charge of the gardens and farms of the late John Wingfield Larkin, at Lee, Kent. The great winter gardens that Mr.Sanders designed here were renowned. The glass structure for the winter gardens was the glass intended for Cairo Railway Station."
>
> Amateur Gardening, October 23rd.,1926

We can try to work out where and when he moved through his apprenticeships as a gardener, by matching some of the circumstantial evidence available in his books, and by the timing of other garden developments between 1868 and 1884.

We know that he had some connection with Messrs.R.Smith & Co. of Worcester who had nurseries spread over two hundred and thirty acres, and employing 300 workers. We also have evidence that he knew of the gardeners at Madresfield Court near Malvern, particularly Mr.Cox, gardener to the Earl

Beauchamp, who introduced a new muscat-flavoured grape in 1868, and Mr.Crump, who introduced a small russet dessert apple.

Later, he had some connections with Messrs.Webb & Son of Wordsley, near Kinver. They had three farms covering 1,600 acres.

Co-incidentally, between 1871 and 1873, Birmingham Botanical Gardens built their Palm House and Terrace Glasshouses.

The Palm House was the largest, rising to a height of twenty-five feet, and housing ferns, palms, and later a Norfolk Island Pine. The Terrace Glasshouses now contain an Orangery which is very much in the style of a Victorian conservatory, with citrus fruits such as oranges, lemons, and limes, and which Sanders would certainly have recognised. He also used photographs of the Botanical Gardens later on in his books.

These four places - Messrs.R.Smith; Madresfield Court; Messrs.Webb; and Birmingham Botanical Gardens - all fit successfully into the possible career path of a new and up-and-coming gardener's assistant with a knowledge of glasshouses.

By the age of nineteen he was working at the Gardens of Versailles. After that, again we have to take circumstantial evidence about where he was placed. Sanders personally stated that it had taken him twelve years of training and then four years of progressing through the ranks before he was ready for garden management.

> "On occasion when he has been a guest at a great house, and has been shown over the gardens, Mr.Sanders surprised his host by his knowledge of their history, and explained that, as a young man, he had designed or actually done the original planting."
>
> Amateur Gardening, October 23rd.,1926

This implies that he was an apprentice from about the age of thirteen until he was twenty-five, and only took on a senior position when he reached the age of thirty. This matches quite closely the date we know - 1884 - when he became a recognised gardening manager for John Wingfield Larkin.

After Versailles, and based on the houses and gardens he used as illustrations in his books later on, he may well have had connections with Clandon Park, near Guildford, (where substantial additional work on the gardens was completed in the late nineteenth century); with Aldenham House, near Elstree; Friar Park, Henley-on-Thames; Nuneham Park Gardens, Oxford; and Watermouth Castle, Ilfracombe.

Whatever his career moves on the way up, it was finally at The Firs - John Wingfield Larkin's property at Lee, in Kent - that Sanders became a leading gardener in 1884.

FROM GARDENER TO PROFESSIONAL 1884-1887

John Wingfield Larkin appointed Thomas Sanders in 1884 to manage "The Firs" at Lee, Kent. Sanders was now a fully fledged gardener. His career was founded on the practical experience he had gained during his apprenticeship. It had lasted sixteen or more years between 1867 and 1884.

Sanders designed the large Winter Garden area. Although the house and its gardens are long gone, swallowed up by what is now Lewisham, photographs, and paintings of the garden by W. Mead, still exist. These show a scene which has a hint of wildness and informality, with plants and shrubs flowing naturally together and through each other, hanging over lawns and pathways. This was very different to the ordered world of the formal gardens of laid-out borders, and decorative knot-gardens, and summer bedding.

He was fairly forthright in his opinions about the traditional formalities:

> "In summer, beds were mainly planted mosaic fashion with coloured-leaved exotics, designated "carpet-bedding," or with circles or bands of brilliantly flowered tender plants like the scarlet, pink, or white geranium, the yellow or brown calceolaria, the purple petunia, and so forth, subjects that had to be reared by the thousands at a great cost by means of artificial heat. The effect of the brilliance of colour thus obtained was magnificent, it is true, but terribly garish and monotonous to the vision. There was no daily change in the contour of the plants, nor in the variation of the colour. You simply gazed upon the same object day after day."
>
> Amateur Gardening, March 17th.1923

Clearly, not his kind of flower borders! And he could be quite cutting about the garden designer dreaming up the arrangements:

"There are gardens and gardens. Those that were considered beautiful during the greater portion of the last century were distinguished more for the genius and skill of the geometrician, the architect, and the sculpture, than for what we should, in these modern times, call true beauty. And added to these severely formal and soulless features, were the equally formal practices which largely prevailed of tree clipping and planting of beds and borders with lines or geometrical patterns of garish tender flowers."

Amateur Gardening, December 7th.,1901

Sanders rejected this lack of the spirit of nature and natural planting, and made it plain when he later became a gardening writer:

"It is manifest that if we wish to have beautiful gardens, we must not only know how to cultivate a garden, but we must also cultivate an artistic perception - a knowledge of the beautiful - to enable us to form beautiful scenes which, collectively, are essential to the attainment of a beautiful garden."

Amateur Gardening, January 1st.,1898

And clearly he felt that:

"The true gardener does not, nowadays, rely upon a labyrinth of fancifully designed beds or elaborately planned paths and terraces to make a beautiful garden, but more upon grouping and massing the great wealth of noble trees or handsome hardy flowers on and around the lawn, so as to obtain the most beautiful effect at all seasons."

Amateur Gardening, December 7th.,1901

He practised what he preached when he was the gardener at

"The Firs", and from the pictures and photographs we get a sense that the borders were a real expression of what he was to write about later on. He might very well have been describing his own work when he said:

> "The outlines of borders, or of walks, should have an easy, flowing curve, not too wriggling or acute, nor quite straight, unless there be a really good reason for it...
>
> The great point is to make the paths, beds, and borders as simple as possible."
>
> Amateur Gardening, September 26th.,1903

At "The Firs" we know that he designed the large Winter Garden area - which in its time became a well-known place for horticulturists to visit. Quite rightly, the recognition these Winter Gardens received, in turn, brought Sanders his own professional recognition.

He was just as clear that winter gardens and conservatories should be as modern in their design as beds and borders:

> "What I am anxious to do in this respect is to endeavour to point out ways and means of arranging the interiors of conservatories so as to partake of the nature of a garden in form and general effect, instead of, as is generally the case, a grocer's shop...
>
> Why should we take infinite pains to arrange our drawing or sitting-rooms with consummate taste and yet be content to have the conservatory usually leading out of such rooms so positively ugly and inartistic in appearance?"
>
> Amateur Gardening, December 16th.,1893

By coincidence the same year, 1884, he started at "The Firs", W.H. & L.Collingridge had appointed Shirley Hibberd to be the first editor of their new weekly magazine "Amateur Gardening."

Shirley Hibberd would have been the natural choice. He had a long and successful career as a writer. By the end of the century he had written a string of botanical and horticultural books. The botanical ones included: 'Field Flowers', 'Brambles and Bay Leaves', 'Wild Flowers through the Seasons', and 'The Seaweed Collector'. The horticultural books included: 'The Fern Garden', 'The Ivy - A Monograph', 'Greenhouse Favourites', 'New and Beautiful-Leaved Plants', 'The Floral World and Garden Guide' 'Familiar Garden Flowers', 'The Amateur's Rose Book', 'The Amateur's Kitchen Garden', 'The Amateur's Flower Garden', 'The Amateur's Greenhouse and Conservatory', and 'Rustic Adornments for Homes of Taste'!

Obviously a prolific and successful writer, it is all the more surprising that Hibberd didn't last long as editor. Within three years he was eased out in preference for T.W.Sanders. This was certainly a sudden and dramatic step to take so early in the magazine's existence.

Clearly something was "not quite right". This is not the place for an assessment of the merits of Shirley Hibberd[1], but it is worth considering why Sanders took over. The management obviously wanted a magazine which could be used by ordinary everyday gardeners, as well as anyone who fancied it as a profession. Maybe Hibberd's style of writing was firmly rooted in the traditions of professional or intellectual gardening, and part of a mid-Victorian outlook. Hibberd's books had heavily embossed and ornate covers, more in keeping with the library than the potting shed, and expecting his readers to have the time, money, intellect and expertise to appreciate his literary gardening.

Rightly or wrongly, we get the sense of Hibberd as a rural horticulturist on an estate. With Sanders we get the sense of a

1. See Ann Wilkinson's "The Preternatural Gardener: The Life of James Shirley Hibberd 1825-1890" Garden History Vol.26.2, 153-175

practical man for the urban terrace or rural cottage garden. Also, when Sanders became a writer and editor he was definitely looking forward towards the start of the twentieth century.

Hibberd's last editorial on April 30th.,1887 was on the topic of pests and diseases. He was somewhat bitter and ambiguous in places:

> "There are people who fail in everything they touch, and there are people who succeed in everything they touch."

But from now on it was T.W.Sanders who would shape "Amateur Gardening" for the next forty years.

EDITING AMATEUR GARDENING 1887-1926

Starting this section of the book was one of the most daunting for me. How do you successfully capture the amount of energy T.W.Sanders showed as editor of 'Amateur Gardening'?

Perhaps it's at least appropriate to start with what was written in his obituary:

> "He exercised the most powerful influence in popular gardening of any writer of his day, and the secret of this lay largely in the fact that he had had unique practical experience of horticulture in all its branches, and of agriculture, too, combined with the natural skill of conveying it to others by his writing. Readers knew that they were getting sound advice in Amateur Gardening."
>
> Amateur Gardening, October 23rd.,1926

As already mentioned, he took over as editor in 1887. During the first few years he established his own writing pattern. This included, obviously, editorials, and also later on some of his own articles and lectures. He also added a week-by-week practical gardening column, and also quite literally pages of "Doubts and Difficulties" which consisted of advice to gardeners on any subject.

> "His letter-bag was extraordinary. Apart from his Amateur Gardening letters - and this meant many thousands of answers a year - he received letters from all over the world, from the African desert, where a lonely Englishman wanted to cultivate some home flowers; to South Sea Islands. Letters came from every walk of life, and peer and peasant received the same treatment from him."
>
> Amateur Gardening, October 23rd.,1926

Consider, he continued to provide editorials, articles, advice, and replies to letters, not just for a few years, but for forty years. Not monthly but every week, a total of over two thousand magazines between 1887 and 1926 without a break.

We know how he did it as well; he would get up at 6.30a.m. regularly to start work at his home office in Embleton Road, Lewisham. Arthur Hellyer recorded that:

> "H.A.Smith (his assistant)...lived nearby,
> walked round daily to work with Sanders and,
> once a week, visited the Collingridge Office
> in London to bring copy and make up for the
> next issue."
>
> Letter to Alan Boon, October 5th.,1990

So far I had the outline features of his work as editor. Now I faced the daunting task of reading two thousand magazines to see what my good friend Sanders had actually produced.

In 1887 and 1888 he was very much engaged on finding a new direction for the magazine. Many of his editorials were nostalgic for the countryside and the cottage gardens he remembered so well. He talked about red valerian in nearly every cottage garden in Worcestershire,

> "the charming beauty of the yellow primrose,
> or the chaste loveliness of the snowdrop,"
>
> Amateur Gardening, February 4th.,1888

> "the beautiful pictures created in spring in
> woodland glades by the snowy white masses of
> the wood anemone."
>
> Amateur Gardening, August 25th.,1888

But by 1889 he seemed to have found his own direction for the magazine. He crossed swords with "The Times" in an editorial on February 2nd.,1889 on fruit growing as a profitable industry, and from then on he showed a more robust side to his writing and a greater commitment to the idea that successful rural horticulture and agriculture had to be based on sound principles and profit.

On November 15th.,1890 he embarked on a series of weekly supplements which would eventually become "An Encyclopaedia of Gardening". After one or two breaks in the spring of 1892 and 1893, it was finally finished on August 31st.,1895, and announced for publication the following week.

During the same period between 1890 and 1895 in addition to his regular features (editorial, week-by-week gardening, and doubts and difficulties) he also wrote articles on "The Profitable Use of Boundary Wall and Fences" (December 19th., and 26th.,1890), "Alpine Plants for Small Gardens" (May 21st.,1892 onwards), "A Garden under Glass" (December 16th.,1893), "A Garden of Roses" (February 17th.,1894), "Grasses Cultivated and Wild" (December 15th.,1894), and "Bulb Culture in the House" (September 7th.,1895).

These are the only articles to which he actually put his name. Throughout his time as editor many articles are frustrating because they were published without an author, or often with a pseudonym. Many were probably by Sanders, but cannot be attributed to him with any certainty.

From July 2nd.,1898 onwards he presented a "Rose Schedule", which in time would become first Piper's "Cultivated Roses" and then his own "Roses and Their Cultivation". In the spring of 1899 his wife was seriously ill, and in May he was ill himself. By the autumn he had recovered enough to start "Profitable Farm and Gardening" , and gave a free copy to readers of "Amateur Gardening" on October 21st.

At the beginning of the new century the magazine was well-settled into its format, with regular features from writers whose work would be published later, and often edited by Sanders. He wrote a short piece on "The Oxlip" in the edition of

October 20th.,1900, and in the Christmas edition of December 8th., he wrote a long article entitled "Eve's Daughters" supporting the potential for women to be independent business managers in horticulture.

In 1901 he wrote a number of additional articles including "The Old-Fashioned Phlox" (March 20th.), "An Old Garden" (June 29th.), "Shading Greenhouses" and "Lilium Tigrinum" (both July 6th.), and then "A Midsummer Garden Scene" as part of his Christmas editorial. "About Walnuts" appeared on August 23rd.,1902. The following year (1903) he announced the first four volumes in the "Profit from the Land" series at the end of May; they were finally published in July and August. Sanders produced a number of articles in the autumn including "School Gardens" (August 8th.), "Old Time Gardens" (August 29th.), "A Garden of Hardy Flowers" (September 26th.), "Beautiful Roses" (November 7th.,) and a quirky end-of-year piece with the fascinating title of "A Chat about Leaf Gall"! By this time he had also been elected as a Fellow of the Linnean Society.

1904 saw Sanders touring in Eire in May, so it was not until late in the year that he turned out a major article - "Our Feathered Friends" - on December 2nd., even with its lighthearted title, still a serious look at the natural food-chain which actually helped gardeners:

> "In birds the farmer and gardener have
> a most valuable ally and friend, whose
> reduction in numbers upsets the balance
> of nature to a serious extent."

On May 6th.,1905 "Amateur Gardening" celebrated its twenty first year. Sanders produced one of his most lively editorials for the occasion, describing different innovations he had introduced, especially "Doubts and Difficulties" in June 1887, the first coloured plate on May 12th.,1888, and the first Christmas number at the end of that year as well.

> "We are proud of our protege, proud of the fact that it has no rival in influence, prestige, popularity, usefulness, or circulation in horticultural journalism in the whole world."
> Amateur Gardening, May 6th.,1905

T.W.Sanders was certainly leaving no room for doubt in the minds of the magazine's readers!

At the end of the year, in the Christmas edition on December 2nd., 1905 he again returned to the theme of the previous year with "Nature in the Garden", supporting the place of Toads, Hedgehogs, Earthworms, Spiders, Ants and Bees, all in the great scheme of things.

In 1906 and 1907 he was taken up with the organisation of major European visits which he reported on extensively in "Profitable Farm and Garden". Clearly he had overstretched himself, because in a remarkably candid article on December 7th.,1907 - "The Welsh Tyrol" - he admitted:

> As the writer of these lines can honestly claim to be a busy man, a hard worker, and a fairly large consumer of the "midnight oil," he, acting upon medical advice, had to choose as the location of his last summer holiday...the mountains of North Wales for obtaining the rest and rejuvenation required."

By this time he seems to have fitted into the format of editorial, seasonable hints, and doubts and difficulties, with only the occasional major article. In 1908 he provided two pieces for the Christmas edition on December 12th., - "Ancient Sundials - The Precursor of Clocks" and "In time of Cherries - Blossom and Fruits". In 1909 he wrote an article on "Winter Flowers" for the edition of March 6th.

In 1910 he returned to a style of reporting visits which he had used in "Profitable Farm and Gardening": "Sweet Peas: A Day with a Cambridge Grower" (January 29th.); in 1911 he repeated the style with "Worcester: Sweet Peas" (January 21st.) and "English Grown Bulbs" (September 30th.). All of these described visits he had made to growers, respectively in Cambridge, Worcestershire and Lincolnshire.

By 1912 he was again 'pushing out his frontiers'. This was the first year of the "Amateur Gardening Year Book" - a collection of major articles and advice for gardeners and horticulturists. He also promoted the formation of the National Hardy Plant Society; he was a Member of the Founding Council, involved with the First Exhibition held at the Royal Horticultural Society on June 19th., and part of the discussions around publishing a Quarterly Journal. In May and June he was also heavily involved in The Royal International Horticultural Exhibition which stretched over twenty seven acres of exhibits and trade at the Royal Military Hospital and Ranelagh Gardens on the Chelsea Embankment.

He finished 1912 with another "natural" article - "Weeds and Their Seeds" - on December 7th. The following year, 1913, he was on his travels again, this time to Bruges, Ghent, and The Ardennes.

The outbreak of The Great War in 1914 forced drastic changes on "Amateur Gardening" and Sanders as its editor. Clearly the call to arms took his younger writers away; by 1915 he was having to write "stand-in" articles, on occasions reprinting earlier material: "Mistletoe: How To Grow It from Seed" (March 13th.), "Rose Enemies and Friends" (June 5th.), "Something about Roses" (June 19th.), "Shading Greenhouses" (July 17th.), "Beautiful Garden Lilies" (July 24th.), "Soldiers' Gardens" (September 25th.) and "Border Carnations" (October 9th.)

He had to admit the loss of the Christmas edition - the Nation was in no mood for lighthearted articles. Over the next three years he was going to be called on to write more and more for the magazine, and take a much greater responsibility for its successful production.

During 1916 he wrote quite extensively for the magazine. On May 6th. he produced a long article entitled "A London City Garden", about the formal gardens at Staple Inn, High Holborn. This was followed by "Whitsun Window Gardening", (May 27th.), "Insect Enemies of the Rose" (June 10th.), "The Art of Exhibiting Roses" (July 1st.), and "Allotment Gardens" (September 9th.) in which he was quite forthright in his opinions:

> "In and around the Metropolis some hundreds of acres have been acquired, laid out, and successfully cropped this season with vegetables that must have proved a source of great help to the cultivators and their families as an appreciable and valuable addition to their food supply. This is a far more commendable and practicable method of encouraging people to grow vegetables than giving the preposterous advice to dig up their flower gardens and convert them into vegetable plots."

He continued with similar themes until the end of the year - "Allotment Gardens" (again, October 21st.), "Food Vegetables" (December 9th.) and "Next Year's Food Crops" (December 30th.)

The first half of 1917 was exactly the same, encouraging people to grow their own produce: "Potatoes - A Warning" (January 20th.), "How to Grow Potatoes" (January 27th.), Utilising Waste Products as Manures" (February 3rd.), "Cropping a War-Time Allotment" (February 24th.) and two editorials - "A Word in Season" (March 3rd.) and "Notes and Comments" (March 10th.). During the autumn, he produced a more varied repertory of articles - "Perennials for Autumn Planting"

(September 22nd.), "How to Grow Cordon Fruit Trees" (October 20th.), "Beautiful Flowering Shrubs" (October 27th.), "A Word to Recruits" (November 10th.) - which was an exhortation about the proper preparation of land for growing vegetables, and "Successful School Gardening" (December 22nd.).

Again, the first half of 1918 was taken up with the growing of vegetables: "Early Vegetables" (January 5th.), "Cultivate! Cultivate!! Cultivate!!!" (March 16th.) - which was intended to help novice gardeners:

> "to lay the foundation for securing really useful food crops to sustain him and his family throughout summer, autumn, winter, and next spring."

March 20th. saw "Special Tips for Food Growers". On April 13th., he published four short articles on "Globe Artichokes", "Purslane", "Useful Summer Food Crops", and "Orache, or Mountain Spinach". He followed this with "Tomato Culture" (April 20th.) and "The Vegetable Oyster" (April 27th.). As before, the second half of the year was more of a mixture: "Herbaceous Phlox" (August 10th.), "Beautifying the Flower Garden" (December 7th.), "Plant Foods" (December 14th.), "Ancient Time-Tellers" (December 21st.) and in the same week "Christmas Thoughts and Greetings":

> "Thank God the hellish wreckage and pillage of homes, the wanton destruction of the land of our Allies, and the murderous slaughter of many thousands of brave men has ceased, never, we hope, to recur."

For the first half of 1919 he maintained the pattern again, but started with a rather different opening - "The Robin" (January 4th.). The growing sequence which came after consisted of "The

Onion" (February 1st.), "Broad Beans" (March 8th.), "Good King Henry" (March 15th.), "Asparagus" and "Spinach Beet" (March 29th.). He then began to turn away from the difficulties being faced, with "A Word to Readers - A Plea for the Flower Garden" (April 5th.):

> "Now the wretched war is over and everyone is trying to settle down as far as possible to pre-war conditions of life, greater attention will, we hope, be paid to the flower garden than has been the case for the last four years."

For the rest of 1919, wrote the introductory articles called "Garden Enemies" which would eventually turn into the book called "Garden Foes" with Kate Ashley's illustrations, combining the three separate works of "Flower Foes", "Fruit Foes" and "Vegetable Foes", and more detailed and complete than the original 1910 edition. The serialisation stopped during the winter because Kate Ashley had died, but eventually restarted in the spring of 1920.

1920 was the first year after the war when a degree of normality appeared to settle on "Amateur Gardening", reflecting the horticultural world in which they worked. Sanders wrote a short article on "Lincolnshire Spinach" (April 10th.). Next he recounted his visit to The Cardiff Show, on July 3rd. There were articles on "Summer Pruning Fruit Trees" (July 24th.), "Our Rose Calendar" (December 4th.) and "Gardening Calendars" (December 25th.).

Apart from his usual material (it is so easy to forget that while he was writing the stand-in articles he was still producing "Doubts and Difficulties", editorials, and weekly hints columns in every magazine, every week), in 1921 he wrote two additional pieces - "Hints on Lime and Fertilisers" (March 12th.) and "Flowering Shrubs for Walls" (September 24th.). He had also completed the outstanding sections and an addendum for "Garden Enemies".

1922 saw him back writing (and to a certain extent reprinting) articles on a whole range of topics. The year started with "Globe Artichokes" (March 25th.), "Purslane" (April 1st.), "Vegetable Garden and Plot - Asparagus" (April 8th.) and "Some Friendly Garden Insects" (April 22nd.), which was really a complimentary piece to go with the "Foes/Enemies" series.

These were followed by "Summer Bedding Plants" (May 20th.):

> "The time will soon be here when owners of gardens will be faced with the question of furnishing their flower beds with gay flowering or foliage plants, so as to make them attractive from June onwards"

And then by a long article - "The Cult of the Clematis" - on July 22nd. He wrote three more short pieces for the magazine: "Garden Friends" (July 29th.), "Lawns and Greens" (October 21st.), and "Witches' Brooms" (November 4th.).

During 1923 he continued on his serene way with "Hardy Herbaceous Borders" (March 17th.), before an editorial celebrating "Our Fortieth Birthday" was less flattering about the first editor Shirley Hibberd:

> "For the first three years it made very little headway, its contents probably failed to appeal to the requirements of the amateur gardening in those days. In the spring of 1887, however, a change occurred in the editorship, and from that time onward to the present the journal gradually advanced in popularity."

The rest of the year saw three more pieces: "Whitsun Gardening"(May 12th.), "Some Rose Diseases" (July 14th.), and

"Garden Enemies" (August 4th.). But his wife's death left the remainder of the year understandably silent.

In 1924 he produced a variety of pieces, first hosting the "Amateur Gardening Prize Photographs" in the New Year edition of January 3rd. He returned to previous themes: "Eastertide Gardening" (March 29th.), "Manures and Fertilizers" (November 1st.) and "Beautiful Garden Lilies" (November 29th.), before finishing the year with a long article: "Fifty Years of Gardening-Our Editor's Reminiscences" on December 13th.

This was in fact not nostalgic but a hard look at the development of natural gardening techniques in the late nineteenth century over the more formal gardens of the mid-century, and also charting the rise and fall of early gardening magazines and journals including "The Gardeners' Magazine" which was the pioneer of all weekly gardening papers, "The Gardeners' Chronicle" which started in 1841, "The Journal of Horticulture", and "The Garden" which appeared in the 1870's and aimed to lead the change towards more natural gardening.

In 1925 he was still producing articles, including "Attractive Borders" (April 11th.), "Potato Blight" and "The Celery Fly" (both June 20th.), and "Fruit and Flower Diseases" (July 11th.). In his editorial on July 25th. he opened with a challenging article "Royal Horticultural Society Amateur Show - Some Criticisms and Suggestions". He was clearly unhappy with the definition of amateur and the direction the show was taking. The end of the year saw the repeat of earlier articles with "Potato and Celery Diseases" (September 26th.) and "The Herbaceous Border" (November 28th.).

1926, his final year as editor, started with "Passing Thoughts" (January 3rd.), before two reprints from earlier years: "The Cult of the Mistletoe" (January 23rd.) and "The Cult of the Clematis" (June 30th.). On May 8th. he wrote his last great article: "Old Time Gardens", describing in a very measured way the history of gardening. On July 10th. he produced a short article: “Celeriac”, and then two short pieces on “Rose Mildew” (July 24th.) and “Rose Aphides” (August 7th.), before a final reprint of “Cordon Fruit Trees” which appeared on October 16th., just a few days after his death.

The last few words of that piece on old time gardens earlier in the last year says very simply what he had achieved in his forty years as editor:

> “A desire gradually evolved for a more natural system, and in due course the change led on to the present-day ideas of making use of the great wealth of flowering and ornamental trees and shrubs, hardy herbaceous plants, and so on........All who love the beautiful in Nature will agree that the modern taste has come to stay. May it be so.
>
> T.W.S.”

EDITING PROFITABLE FARM AND GARDEN 1899-1913

The Journal began its life on October 21st.,1899. T.W.Sanders was the inaugural editor, and remained with the journal until its demise on February 22nd.,1913.

In the opening editorial - "Money out of the Land" - Sanders described the challenge facing agriculture as it moved from cereal production to the intensive cultivation of different cash crops:

> "The old order is rapidly being superseded by the new, and there is every prospect of the land of this country being made to yield far greater profits than were obtainable in days gone by."
>
> October 21st.,1899

During the first year Sanders contributed a number of articles, beginning with a dislocated series entitled "Among the Growers". The first was an interview with an Essex market gardener, then with a Somerset grower, followed by reports on a Kentish fruit nursery. After a significant gap "A Day in East Anglia - An Interview with Mr.Rider Haggard" appeared. Rider Haggard lived at Ditchingham House near Bungay in Norfolk. Earlier that year he had published his own work - "A Farmer's Year" - which may well have prompted the visit from Sanders, and subsequently the long article in the magazine as a minor journalistic 'coup'.

Apart from that, in the editorials T.W.Sanders set out the principles underpinning the journal.

> "The more widely its aims and objects become known, the greater will be the chances of success in getting people back to the land, the more prosperous and thriving will the rural districts become."
>
> October 20th.,1900

He returned to this theme time and time again in the first three years:

> "Thousands of persons who a few years ago left the picturesque villages of this country for the over-crowded cities and towns are yearning to get back again to engage in the more pleasant pursuit of cultivating the soil."
>
> January 5th.,1901

Maybe he was also thinking about his own situation when he said that people living in London

> "were originally country bred, but left the simple rural surroundings of their birth-place for the gaiety and brighter financial prospects of the city. They have tasted the sweets and the bitters of the latter, have grown tired of both, and now yearn for a return to the more prosaic and peaceful life of the country."
>
> November 16th.,1901

In the first three years from 1899 and 1901 Sanders also referred back to his early days in Worcestershire. He specifically mentioned oast houses near Tenbury Wells in an article on growing fruit against walls. He also spoke at an Exhibition Conference held in Worcester in the Autumn of 1900. He concentrated on the production of cider and perry, making the telling statement that

> "if fruit growing is to be made profitable only the very best sorts should be grown, and the Worcestershire farmer will be well advised to bear this fact in mind."
>
> November 10th.,1900

He also commented on the French Crab Apple, or Winter Greening:

> "This grand old apple is not so generally grown as its merits deserve. I have seen some fine specimen trees in the older Worcestershire orchards."

But he could also be critical about his home county and its growers. He was plain and forthright about the production of currants:

> "If planted on upland slopes and allowed to become smothered with weeds, as we saw several plantations in The Teme Valley, Worcestershire, this season, the trees will be miserable, weak, and stunted specimens, a prey to insects, and an unprofitable crop generally."

After 1902 T.W.Sanders took a more "hands-off" approach to his editorship. By then there were many established agricultural writers who provided the journal with a steady stream of specialist pages on all aspects of farming and smallholding week by week. Later many of these would be turned into practical handbooks for smallholders.

Sanders' contribution consisted of long and detailed reports on visits to different countries which were then serialised over a number of weeks. They are a fascinating record.

In 1903 Sanders recorded in great detail his experiences in Normandy from May 16th. to May 23rd., as part of The British Dairy Farmers'Association visit to France. They all set off from Victoria on Saturday, and crossed from Newhaven to Dieppe. There were 120 participants, and they clearly made some impact when they arrived en masse in France.

"Our party appeared to be a source of great attraction to the Dieppe folk; they not only congregated in hundreds on the quai, but also lined up in great numbers by the side of the train. They evidently meant to get a good idea of what a British farmer was like."

The party travelled by special train to Paris (and throughout the journey on the following days). Sanders made notes about the countryside and properties he saw on the way:

"I cannot say that I admire the French chateaus, or residencies of the wealthier classes. Although generally embosomed in a wealth of trees, they nearly all lacked gardens. The house had the appearance of standing in the midst of a field with not a single flower-bed or shrub to relieve the bareness of the ground, or a creeper to soften or tone down the glaring white and red colours of the walls, doors, and windows. There was a suggestion of bareness and desolation."

The party stayed at the Hotel Central in Paris. The following day, Sunday, Sanders went sightseeing, visiting Napoleon's Tomb, The Louvre, The Tuileries, Salon, and Notre Dame. He also managed to fit in a visit to the markets of Les Halles.

His comments about Parisians were less than enthusiastic!

"I mention for the benefit of readers who may contemplate visiting Paris for the first time, that it is a Britisher's privilege to be fleeced right and left unless he is

> exceedingly careful. The hotels, cafes, and the shop people will endeavour to charge you double or treble the ordinary value, or to give you short change."

After the Paris experience - it also poured with rain! - Sanders was in a more optimistic mood when they all departed on Monday for Plaisir-Grignon, where they visited the French National School of Agriculture. On the way back they stopped at The Palace of Versailles (where Sanders had been a gardening apprentice). They travelled by horse drawn carriage and Sanders observed:

> "Through the villages the inhabitants turned out en bloc, gazing with wonderment as to who we were, and where we were going. In all cases, however we were saluted with great respect, and only in one instance did I observe one "gamin" practise the bad habit of his English confrere - rudely extend his digits from his nasal organ."

Back in Paris, the day ended with a Formal Dinner with speeches and toasts from both countries.

On Tuesday they were off to Chaumont-en-Vexin where they visited a dairy, on to Vernon, and then by road to Pressagny.

> "The ride was a delightful one as regards scenery, but not so far as personal comfort was concerned. The roads were fearfully dusty, and the fact of our retinue consisting of some twenty or more vehicles, ancient and modern, did not improve matters."

At Pressagny they visited a cheese factory producing Camembert and Coulommiers, before travelling via Vernon to Rouen.

On Wednesday they set off down the Seine by steamer, Sanders declaring:

> "It was a glorious day for the journey, the breeze coming down the water being sufficient to temper the fierceness of the heat."

They were supposed to put in at Caudebec but unfortunately the engine bearings overheated. After running repairs they steamed straight through to Honfleur where they caught their special train to Le Breuil-Blangy, again to see cheese production.

On Thursday they set off from Caen to Bayeux where Sanders visited the Cathedral, the Bayeux Tapestry, and the old black-and-white timbered houses in Rue St.Martin. In the afternoon they set out by horse-drawn carriage to Sully for an afternoon of farm and dairy tours ending up at Monceaux.

Friday was a conference day in Caen. Sanders made an early start with a visit to the street cattle market first. The main conference speaker was Professor Leze, from The National School of Agriculture, who spoke on the production of milk, cream, butter and cheese in France. In the afternoon they were all off again to visit a butter-blending plant at St.Pierre-sur-Dives. Sanders noted the production methods with some disquiet:

> "The butter is thrown into the mould by hand and pressed in, then squared off level at the top, and finally released from the mould ready to pack into boxes. I cannot say that the method of preparing the Normandy butter is an over-inviting one. The operators who handle it had a by no means cleanly appearance, and I do not think I shall relish this otherwise excellent butter so well in future."

Saturday saw them on a visit to a moated chateau at Victor-Pontfol. On the way Sanders commented on the Normandy countryside:

> "The scenery impressed me as being very English in character, such as one meets with in Devon, Gloucester, and Worcester. The fields were small, and enclosed with neat hedgerows, the pasturage rich, and plentifully sprinkled with buttercups and meadow flowers, and the fruit orchards numerous, and in splendid condition. Here and there we passed some very old half-timbered cottages, with ample gardens attached, and gay with the blossoms of the rose."

After a champagne break, they were off to Mezidon, posing at the railway station for a formal photograph. The last night was spent at Rouen where at the final dinner they regaled each other with patriotic songs and speeches for each country.

A final visit to Rouen Cathedral, and witnessing a religious procession to the monument of Joan of Arc at the Church of Bonsecours, then the next morning a rough crossing took them all back to Newhaven and London.

1904 saw Sanders on his travels again with a visit to Eire, touring Wicklow, Tipperary, Cork, and Limerick. The most important engagement he kept was at a Conference and Exhibition held at Ball's Bridge Dublin, at the invitation of The Department of Agriculture. he had some misgiving about the need to go. However, once he saw the exhibits, he was in a more positive frame of mind:

> "After a first glance at the magnificent display of brilliant coloured fruit, staged in an equally noble building..staged on snowy-white tables, gracefully draped with an emerald green

fringe, the effect was most pleasing to the eye."

Sanders was surprised to discover that the Show had been organised at very short notice to ensure that entries would be "naturally" produced, not forced or selected. The Conference day was attended by growers from all over Eire. The top fruits in discussion were apples, plums, damsons, pears, and cherries. It is interesting that in reporting the speeches Sanders showed that preferential (and unfair) support had been given to fruit-growing in what is now Northern Ireland.

Other issues covered included selective culture, grading and packing, and effective marketing.

The following year (1905) he reported extensively on a visit to Holland he had organised in late May for a group of journalists interested in agriculture and horticulture. On arrival Sanders noted with a hint of dry humour:

> "The Customs officials were a very civil lot of fellows, asked few questions, and did not seem to show quite the same amount of minute inquisitiveness that our own officials did when we landed at London on our return."

As you might expect they spent a significant part of their tour inspecting dairy farms and the production of dairy products, particularly Gouda and Edam cheese, and Dutch butter. But there was also time for Sanders to take in some of the garden perspectives of the country. In The Hague they visited the Haagsche Bosch - a wood on the edge of the city.

> "The trees are mostly beech, with straight, clear stems fifty feet or more high, and dense heads towering seventy feet or more in the air."

And he also noticed the style of domestic gardens around the houses they passed:

> "The Dutch folk are very partial to coloured foliage, and hence in every garden one saw either beds of Japanese maples, or large trees of purple beech, or silver maple freely dotted about."

Wherever they went in Holland they were given a resounding welcome, especially in The Hook of Holland.

> "Many hundreds of Dutch farmers and market gardeners had assembled and gave us all a rousing reception. We were besieged by the latter enquiring in good or broken English our opinion of their products,"

and en route they found that in the larger villages all the school children and locals turned out en masse to get a look at them. Over the course of the week they travelled extensively in the provinces of Zuid-Holland, Noord-Holland, and Friesland, reaching as far as Leeuwarden in the north, where their visit culminated in a formal banquet given in their honour by the Provincial Government of Friesland.

The next year - 1906 - it was the turn of Shropshire to receive The British Dairy Farmers'Conference, and again Sanders was a leading member and reporter of the event. There was a hint of nostalgia in the way Sanders described their visit - he was not that far from his home county of Worcestershire.

> "On our way we noted several charming villages and pretty rural homesteads, each having a large garden attached and fringed with a number of the far-famed Shropshire damson trees, which in the days of our youth were wont to yield a substantial sum yearly....In those days the fruit was in much demand.. Many a cottager made a £5 note easily."

After a Civic Reception in Shrewsbury, the following days were spent in the north and west of the County visiting farms and also training colleges. Sanders gave particular prominence to the Shropshire Technical School for Girls at Radbrook - he had always championed the right of woman to equality of opportunity and employment.

Apart from the farm and colleges he highlighted the Whitchurch Cheese Fair (then a monthly event). The following tour seems to have involved a series of dairy farms and dinners, with a special interest shown in Woodlands Farm at Bicton, Hardwicke Grange, The Twemloes, Park Hall at Oswestry, and Otterley Park at Ellesmere.

The final series of reports for the journal appeared in the summer of 1906, arguably the most important and successful visit with which Sanders had been involved. He had been formally invited by the Government of Sweden to lead a delegation to the National Agricultural Show at Norrkoping, and then to a tour through the agricultural districts of Southern Sweden in late June and early July.

They departed from Tilbury on the S.S.Thorsten, in high spirits and with an accompanying Smorgasbord banquet washed down with schnapps and lager. The North Sea though was decidedly stormy; even Sanders admitted that:

> "The writer has to humbly confess that he was one of those that had to seek refuge in his cabin, and there he had to remain most unwillingly...for thirty-six hours....So long as he laid down all was well, but the moment the head was lifted then trouble began."

Eventually tea and dried toast, with calmer weather off the Danish coast, restored him and the rest of the party. When they arrived in Gothenburg Sanders was surprised by what he saw:

> "We noticed that the trees, the vegetation, and even the crowd of folks sauntering along.. had a distinctly British look about them. The oak, the ash, the birch, and the lime were the chief trees...We recognised, also, many of our familiar birds."

After a nine-hour train journey and an overnight in Norrkoping, they were escorted to a special stand not far from the Royal dais, from which King Oscar opened the Show and presented the major awards to exhibitors. In the evening the King, together with Princess Margaret of Connaught (then Princess Adolphus of Sweden) entertained the British party to a Royal Dinner.

> "We spent a long time conversing with our hosts, who seemed to take a great delight in conversing in English with us....Every one seemed eager to make us happy."

By the third day they were on their travels to Linkoping, first stopping at a Horticultural School near Atvidaberg and then spending the afternoon at a Swedish Model Farm at Bjarka Saby. They then all moved on to Stockholm. Arriving at the Grand Hotel facing the Royal Palace, Sanders experienced his first sauna, during which he was surprised by:

> "The entrance of a buxom woman of by no means tender years and powerful muscles. This Amazon was armed with a big brush and a bar of soap, and she proceeded straightaway to give us a sound scrubbing.....It appears to be the custom in Sweden to do this sort of thing."

After this traditional early morning greeting, they set off on factory and farm visits around the capital.

> "The journey (to Saltsjobaden) was by water through a series of charming lakes picturesquely undulated and clothed with spruce fir. A more delightful spot could not be imagined. The hill slopes were dotted with pretty villas, large and small, and the lakes broken up here and there with small islands. In many places the water was very shallow, and as clear as crystal."

On Sunday they had a more informal time at the Skansen Open-Air Museum, before taking an overnight train to Malmo. The local consul gave them a full variety of experiences there with visits to a butter-testing centre, and the city slaughter-house, followed on the next day with an experimental seed farm, a pig-breeding centre, and the Alnarp Agricultural Institute.

Their final day was spent at a baronial farm estate at Nasbyholme before travelling overnight again back to Gothenburg for a last sauna, and a final celebration party with the Swedish Ministry of Agriculture

The return crossing, on the S.S.Thule, was plagued by fog, but at last they pulled into Tilbury. Clearly their visit had been designed to establish stronger economic ties between Sweden and Britain, especially for the import of high quality dairy products such as butter. The fact is that the King of Sweden had been in contact with the party not just at the Norrkoping, but by telegram on their last night in Malmo indicating its importance, and subsequently Sanders was honoured by being created a Knight (First Class) of the Royal Order of the Vasa for his support for Sweden's agricultural and horticultural industries.

Strangely, this was the last major article Sanders wrote for the journal. As I mentioned before, it had a group of well-established writers providing regular copy week by week. In some ways, looking at it from a century's distance, the journal seems to have become stuck in a familiar, almost tedious rut.

Finally, its copyright was given up to "The Smallholder", a magazine with similar and overlapping interests, and on February 22nd., 1913, with little or no comment, Sanders relinquished his editorship.

A MAN FOR ALL GARDENING: T.W.SANDERS AS SPEAKER

From almost the first day he became editor of 'Amateur Gardening' Sanders made a very real and practical commitment to support gardening organisations, both national and local.

His greatest contribution was as the founder of The National Amateur Gardeners Association. It was first announced on December 27th.,1890. The first meeting was to be held at the Corn Exchange Tavern in the City, where on January 13th.,1891 a Provisional Committee was formed with Sanders as President.

The first constituted meeting took place on March 3rd. at The Guildhall Tavern in Gresham Street. Sanders gave the inaugural talk on "Root Stocks for Roses", declaring one of his favourite roses was Aimee Vibert. Again, on April 7th., he led a discussion on "Best Plants for Amateurs to Grow" (if you wish to follow his advice, then you will grow the Chinese Fan Palm, Australian Silky Oak, Araucaria imbricata, Aralia japonica, Dracaena australis, Primula obconica, pelargoniums and fuchsias!) In October 1891 Sanders lectured again on "Heating Small Greenhouses".

The new association also began to organise visits. Over the year they went off to Barr's and Sons Daffodil Nurseries at Long Ditton, Ware's Nursery near Tottenham, Cannell and Sons near Swanley, Sutton and Sons of Reading, Paul and Sons at Waltham Cross, Kew Botanical Gardens, H.J.Jones of Lewisham, and Cheal and Sons of Crawley (for which The London, Brighton, and South Coast Railway offered a special fare of a two shillings, five-and-a-half pence!)

The first Annual Dinner attracted 80 people, and in 1892 they were established so successfully they moved to the Memorial Hall in Farringdon Street. Other Branch Societies had formed during the year: in Liverpool, Reading, and Exeter; Birmingham joined the year after; three other Societies affiliated: The Ladywell and District Cottagers, The New Cross Amateur Gardeners, and - a surprise - The Tasmanian Amateur Gardeners'Association! By 1894, Associations in Gosport, Charlton, Forest Hill, Highbury,

J. Collingridge Esq
T.W. Sanders Esq
Mr Cuthbertson
Dobbie & Son.
Wm Sydenham Esq
S. Rashleigh Esq
Mr Holday is very successful.
Bravo! Bedford
Mr G.M. Gross
H.T. Wooderson Esq
G. Gordon Esq
H. Hillman Esq
F. Finch Esq
A.C. 1027

and Neasden had joined up. By this time the NAGA was flourishing so well under Sanders' leadership that at the AGM in February 1893 he was accorded the honour of a Fellowship of the Association.

Sanders kept up his talks to the Association, acting as a regular speaker - in 1894 "Vegetable Culture", 1895 "Hardy Perennials", 1896 "The Culture of Hardy Bulbs", and memorably 1900 when on May 1st. he gave an impromptu lecture on "Tomato Culture" when the guest speaker failed to turn up!

Clearly the Association was quite a sociable group. Every year they held their Annual Dinner, and in 1895 they branched out to hold what was called a "Conversazione" of songs, music, and recitals by members and friends. 400 attended, so from then on it became an annual summer event; more than 500 "gardeners and friends" turned up the following year, and in 1897 they took over the Royal Botanic Society grounds in Regents Park, with two bands, and Sir Andrew Clarke, Agent-General for Victoria Australia, as the main guest. 3,000 "gardeners and friends" arrived! Year on it continued, and, although not reaching such a crowd again, regularly 500 or more would turn up to a summer venue in London.

By this time the organisation appeared to have both a national and international status - Seapoint Horticultural Society, Capetown, affiliated in 1896; in the same year they had set up a quarterly journal - "Amateur World of Horticulture", and in 1897 created their own members' library. In 1907 they were invited to visit the Royal Gardens at Windsor Castle, and Frogmore House (the home of the then Prince of Wales); in 1911 their summer show was held at Alexandra Palace. By 1912 they were celebrating their 22nd.Anniversary Dinner and Bohemian Concert at the Holborn Restaurant.

Most gardening organisations responded to the outbreak of The Great War in 1914 by disbanding, and the NAGA followed.

After the war, and with Sanders fully committed to re-establishing 'Amateur Gardening' the Association was naturally superseded by local gardening societies all over the country.

This was not the sum total of Sanders' commitment. As well as playing a full part as NAGA President, he supported many other organisations by judging at shows and lecturing at meetings. In August 1889 he judged at the Buxted Flower Show, presenting a bound volume of 'Amateur Gardening' as one of the prizes. He always made a point of returning to judge at the Spring and Summer Shows in Martley (A First Edition of "An Encyclopaedia of Gardening" was a first prize for one lucky winner in 1895!). In 1904 he opened the Charlton Show, and judged regularly for the New Barnet Amateur Gardeners' Association. Just before the outbreak of war he also judged at the Dalston Young People's Society Show.

In 1891, he was key speaker at a forum on gardening issues held jointly by three Croydon gardening societies. He also lectured at the Beddington and Carshalton Fruit Conference on "The Profitable Use of Boundary Walls and Fences". In 1893 he gave a lecture on "First Principles of Horticulture" in Chingford, and "Garden Soils: Their Properties and Methods of Improvement" in Hertford.

In 1899 he gave talks on "Mistakes in Rose Culture" in New Barnet, and "Workers' Gardens" at the National Cooperative Festival and Flower Show.

We know that he was elected to the National Chrysanthemum Society Committee on February 19th.,1894, and quickly rose through its ranks to Vice-Chairman, and Chairman in 1897. During 1898 he resigned (it is not clear why), but at the AGM in February 1899 he was presented with a large gold medal of the Society, and with a decorated scroll address

"This address together with the large
gold medal of the Society is presented to

> Mr.T.W.Sanders, for some years Vice-Chairman and afterwards Chairman of the Executive Committee, as a token of warm personal esteem, and in grateful recognition of the invaluable services rendered to the Society as one of its principal executive officers."
>
> Edwin Saunders, President
> Richard Dean, Secretary

At the same time he was elected as an Honorary Fellow and as Vice-President.

He also supported The National Rose Society and The National Sweet Pea Society, almost always attending their Annual Shows. On at least one occasion he brought H.Bartlett, the NSPS Secretary up to a Martley Garden Show to act as a judge - much to Bartlett's pleasure apparently.

He was known for his steadfast support for The Cooperative Horticultural Exhibitions, attending, judging, and reporting on the Shows. He was an examiner for the Horticultural College at Swanley in Kent, where he noted that generally women students were far better at theory than men, but that often the practice of horticulture showed the reverse to be true.

Sanders was a supporter of the Lady Warwick Agricultural Association for Women, which was founded in 1899. It had three hostels for trainee women near Reading, presumably connected to Whiteknights Park. He spoke at their early meetings, firstly at an informal "drawing-room" event on May 22nd.,1900, when he talked about the marketing of horticultural and agricultural produce by women. He advised them to concentrate on the creation of special markets for produce needed locally.

He spoke at their 2nd.Annual Meeting held at Stafford House, London on October 12th.,1900, again on the theme of fruit and flower growing as a working occupation for women. His view was that:

> "There was no reason whatsoever why women, properly trained and with some start-up capital, could not make flower and fruit growing, with poultry and beekeeping, a profitable and successful industry."

As well as a supporter of all those connected with agriculture and horticulture he was an active, well-established and recognised figure locally in Lewisham where he lived. In 1912 he was elected as a Conservative Town Councillor for Lewisham Park Ward (maybe he liked the green reference!) He served on the Libraries Committee, and was its Chairman from 1915 to 1918, when he resigned from the Council due to ill-health, possibly one of the bouts of bronchitis which seemed to dog him towards the end of his life.

Sanders was also a Freemason. He was one of the founders of the Philanthic Lodge, and in 1893 he was Master of the Caxton Lodge.

With all his connections with Lewisham and work with London publishing, Sanders still showed his affection for his village, presenting Martley Horticultural Society with a set of gardening books by various authors. There were at least thirty-two in the collection, each with his presentation plate on the flyleaf, and numbered on the spine. One lone copy was discovered under the floorboards of the old Village Hall when it was demolished.

The story of all he did is still incomplete, but even from what is recorded here it is clear that he had an almost boundless energy for his chosen profession and for helping anyone who needed his support or advice. 'The Gardeners' Chronicle' said that:

> "no matter how insignificant or foolish a question might appear it was always answered in the kindliest fashion."

FROM CALENDAR TO ALPHABET: T.W.SANDERS AS WRITER

From 1887 until his death in 1926 T.W.Sanders wrote a total of thirty-eight books, and edited at least a further thirty. In that time he covered almost every aspect of gardening and smallholding.

It's very easy to forget that he wasn't just writing and editing books but was just as involved with editing two journals, giving talks and lectures, travelling this country and Europe, judging, and supporting gardening societies. The word "prolific" doesn't do him justice really.

In 1887 he published his first work - "The Garden Calendar", described as:

> "Being a practical guide to the cultivation of fruits, flowers and vegetables during each month of the year."

It was dedicated to his employer J.W.Larkin, and was published by Hamilton Adams & Co.,of London in February, one of the only occasions when he did not use W.H.&L.Collingridge (the publishers of "Amateur Gardening"). We can assume this was a key work which brought him the editorship in the same year at the end of April.

Most of his early books after that started as compilations of articles generated week by week in the journals he wrote for and edited. Many were remarkably short and compact - definitely for the gardener's jacket pocket or greenhouse shelf, not for the library. Only in later editions were they reissued as full size, bound books.

As you might expect the early cheap card-covered editions did not survive the rigours of the potting shed and real gardening. In true Sanders' style they were designed for that. Side-by-side with seeds, bulbs, tubers, and potting compost it does not take much imagination to understand how quickly these little guides would be used to destruction!

His first writing period after 1887 can loosely be dated between 1895 and 1899. In 1895, after weekly episodes between November 15th.,1891 and August 31st.,1895 in 'Amateur Gardening', he announced the publication of "An Encyclopaedia of Gardening".

This was undoubtedly his greatest achievement. During his lifetime and after, it was a key reference work for amateur and professional gardeners alike. So much so, that by the time of his death a quarter of a million copies had been sold in nineteen different editions.

It continued to be revised and republished by the editors who followed him - A.J.Macself and A.G.L.Hellyer - in a twenty-second and twenty-third edition right up to 1976. It was such an important reference work that it was presented in many different adaptations - economy, war-time, de-luxe, matching binding. It is difficult for us to imagine any other non-fiction work with such a practical and domestic theme having such a long, continuous, and significant literary position for more than eighty years, even reaching the bookcase of such well-known presenters as Alan Titchmarsh.

During the same period Sanders also revised three books by the previous editor, Shirley Hibberd: "Rustic Adornments for Homes of Taste" (1895), in which he declared that:

> "It has been necessary to thoroughly revise the original matter, and bring many chapters up to date. new chapters have been introduced, in which floral decorations for interiors, table decorations, plant propagation for amateurs, and the Alpine garden are severally dealt with."

He also revised "The Amateur's Flower Garden" and "The Amateur's Greenhouse and Conservatory" in 1897. In 1899 he edited Weguelin's "Carnations, Picotees, and Pinks" and Piper's

"Cultivated Roses", an alphabetical list of all species and varieties of roses recorded being grown in this country, in itself a fascinating source of information about roses at the turn of the last century. Later Sanders reissued it under his own authorship as "Roses and Their Cultivation".

His second period of writing produced a significant number of what we might now call "Handy Guides" for gardeners and smallholders. "Roots, Bulbs and Tubers for Profit" was edited in 1903, and later expanded under his authorship to "Root Crops - Potatoes, Onions, Beet, Parsnips, Carrots, Turnips, and Other Roots and Tubers". A companion pocket guide also appeared - "Green Crops and Herbs for Profit". This too was later expanded by Sanders to become "Green Crops - Broccoli, Cabbage, Herbs, Etc."

In 1904 he produced "Mushrooms, Cucumbers, Salads, Tomatoes, Etc." and "Asparagus, Beans, Peas, Rhubarb, Seakale, Marrows, Etc." To keep smallholders well on the way to profit the series continued with "Rabbits for Profit and Pleasure" (by Bird), and "Pigs for Profit" (by Walker). In time these were followed by a whole series of edited works: "Fowls for Profit" , "Chicken Rearing and Incubation" and "Duck, Geese, and Turkeys for Profit" (all by Tysilio Johnson), and "Bees for Profit" (by Geary). By the time the pocket series was completed in 1910 there were fifteen mini-volumes.

Sanders also took good care of the gardener as well as the smallholder. In 1902 he wrote "Laying out a Garden and Grounds", and in 1904 he produced a completely new work, "The Amateur's Greenhouse: A Complete Guide to the Construction, Heating, and Management of Greenhouse" which replaced the earlier one by Hibberd.

He wrote two short works for the cottage garden - "Annuals"(1904) and "Perennials" (1905). Together with "Easily Grown Hardy Perennials" by Vos, and edited by Sanders, they ran to three editions before Sanders rewrote them himself later on. "Roses and Their Cultivation" appeared as a revision of Piper's earlier work. In time it became one of Sanders' major achievements, running to fourteen editions by 1931.

"Vegetables and Their Cultivation" also appeared in 1905 and was just as popular, running to seven editions by 1928. He wrote "The Book of the Potato" in the same year, drawing on articles in 'Amateur Gardening' and responding to the active trading going on in new potato hybrids at the time. Lastly, he also found time to edit Crane's "Chrysanthemums for Garden and Greenhouse".

If we pause for a few moments, and look back at these four years between 1902 and 1905, we have just seen Sanders produce eleven books and edit another ten. What an output! Whilst no-one would try to claim that the smaller pamphlets and handy-guides were major inspirational works, more importantly they were accessible (and cheap) - every gardener and smallholder could have one if they wanted to.

After returning from a series of overseas visits, Sanders began to publish his third round between 1907 and 1908. Two major works appeared for the first time: "The Alphabet of Gardening", which ran to eight editions up to 1926; and "The Flower Garden, Its Design, Formation, Planting, and Management", which ran to six editions by 1935, and was then reprinted many times after that.

Two more short guides were written: "Roses" and "Allotments". In 1908 he completed "Bulbs and Their Cultivation, including lists of all the genera, species, and varieties worth growing in The British Isles". There's confidence for you!

He edited two further works: Crane's "Pansies and Violets", and Lansdell's "Grapes and How to Grow Them". After three editions they became joint authors of an expanded book, "Grapes, Peaches, Melons, and How to Grow Them", strangely with the spine of the book showing only Sanders as author. J.Lansdell worked as an Assistant Horticultural Instructor for Worcestershire

County Council. It is quite probable that they had known each other for some time, and may have judged local shows together.

Between 1910 and 1913 Sanders continued to produce a wide range of books on gardening and smallholding, still able to discover new specialist topics to bring to the attention of the amateur gardener.

For the smallholder, he continued to edit short handy guides, including "The Goat, Its Use and Management" (by Bird), "The Horse, Its Care and Management" (by Fawcus), "Sheep, Their Management and Breeding" (by Muir), "Dairy Cows and the Dairy" (by Walker), and his own work - "The Small Holder's Guide: A Manual dealing with the subject of small holdings and their successful management".

For the salad gardener, "Mushrooms and Their Cultivation" arrived in 1910, soon followed by "Salads and Their Cultivation" in 1911, and "Tomatoes and How to Grow Them" which became another best seller, running to eight editions by 1932. Salads need rich soil with a good heart, so it was no surprise to find Sanders editing "Manure for Garden and Farm Crops" by Dyke.

For the gardener more interested in leisure pursuits than laying out vegetables, pleasure rather than profit, Sanders then produced "Lawns and Greens: Their Formation and Management. Garden, Tennis and Croquet Lawns, Bowling and Golf Greens, Cricket Grounds, Grass Paths", giving every sporting gardener the advice and opportunity to create their own ultimate playing surface!

For the more domestic gardener, he wrote "Small Gardens", and "Window and Indoor Gardening" which was separated into two smaller works, "Window Gardens" and "Indoor Gardens" in 1913.

For the gardener, town or country, Sanders wrote "Carnations, Picotees and Pinks" in 1911, updating Weguelin's earlier work. He edited Harrison's "Orchids for Amateurs", and Jenkins' "Rock Gardens and Alpine Plants" which he would expand into a much more important work five years later.

And for the new gardener, and almost at the end of this period of work, he edited Hyde's "School Gardening", possibly as a passing recognition of his own experience in Martley. "School Gardening" was described as:

> "A Simple Book for teaching Boys and Girls in Elementary Schools the Rudiments of Practical Horticulture."

Originally, it had been published in 'Amateur Gardening' in 1912 as a prize-winning article. Hyde was a teacher in Essex, and Sanders encouraged him to turn it into a complete book.

Finally Sanders produced "Garden Foes, Insect, Animal and Fungoid Pests. With all the latest remedies for their eradication." This feisty little volume was published with an ornate cover depicting a fruit bush surrounded and threatened by marauding moths, butterflies, and snails. There are two caterpillar rampant on the lower stems. The picture is bordered with a decorative motif of tendrils and caterpillars, whilst across the foot of the cover marches a formal line of eelworms!

During his next period of writing between 1915 and 1917 Sanders created four major works, all of which were to become established reference works for many years afterwards.

In 1915 he published "Fruit and Its Cultivation" which ran to five editions by 1940 and was still being reissued for some time after that. In 1916 "Rock Gardens and Alpine Plants, Including Water, Bog, and Moraine Gardens" came out as an expansion of the one by Jenkins in 1911. The same year saw another major work - "Popular Hardy Perennials" which in turn became a standard work for five editions. Finally in 1917 "Allotment and Kitchen Gardens" was published. It was continuously edited and reissued, and was still going strong in 1939. And as a response to what must have seemed the never-ending demands of The Great

War, in 1917 he compiled a two-part manual called “Practical Books on Food Production”.

In what was his final period of creative writing between 1921 and 1924 he expanded his “Garden Foes” into three separate volumes entitled “Fruit Foes: Pests that attack fruit trees”, “Vegetable Foes - Insect, animal and fungoid pests”, and “Flower Foes”. All three works were illustrated by Kate Ashley, and came from a long series of articles and illustrations which had previously been published in ‘Amateur Gardening’. Later, in 1929, they were rebound into a single volume called “Garden Foes” under the direction of A.J.Macself .

His last work, strangely late in his writing, was “Annual Flowers for Garden and Greenhouse”. He spent the last two years reworking new editions, especially “The Alphabet of Gardening” which was printed in a gold-and-black ‘mourning edition’ in February 1927.

After his death, four small books were issued by A.J.Macself under his authorship as ‘The Popular Handbook Series’- “Roses”, “Sweet Peas”, “Violas and Pansies”, and “Chrysanthemums”. In the last one, dated 1925, Sanders quoted from a poem by Hicks:

> “Yet I would weep no tears, nor mate with sorrow,
> But glow with love, and hope a glad to-morrow,
> Drink joy, and, fearless of impending doom,
> Brave life’s grey shadows with a burst of bloom”

T.W.SANDERS
EPILOGUE
AND
ONE CENTURY ON

The combination of optimism and stoicism Sanders showed in that last passage of poetry match the last few years of his life, which were stressful and traumatic.

In 1921 he was suffering from a bout of bronchitis, but was still carrying on with as much energy as he could, wanting to come up to the Summer Show in Martley, his home village.

But two years later his wife Annie died in 1923, and by his own admission by 1926 he was finding the task of revising and editing increasingly burdensome:

> "I have had a very anxious and arduous time to go through the last two months. So many of my books have run out of sale and I am busily engaged on bringing them up to date, which means much concentration of thought and hard work."
>
> Letter to Mrs.Fidoe, Martley, July 28th.,1926

The handwriting in his last letter to her shows that he is clearly unwell; the writing curves away, and the script lacks the control of a steady hand, but even then he still wanted to keep on his travels, planning to come up to Worcester.

Sadly within three months T.W.Sanders was dead, struck down by pneumonia. Most of the revisions he did not live to see in print. The last was an eighth edition of "The Alphabet of Gardening", which he finished with the words of the poet Cowper:

> "To study culture, and with artful toil
> To 'meliorate and tame the stubborn soil;
> To give dissimilar yet fruitful lands
> The grain, the herb, the plant that each demands;
>
> ....
>
> These, these are arts pursued without a crime
> That leave no stains upon the wings of Time."

At his funeral the Vicar of Lewisham, the Rev.A.L.Preston, said:

> "Here was a man who, from the very beginning, had a vocation; he had a vocation for beauty. He considered the flowers of the field, the things of the earth, and behind these things he saw something of the beauty of God. So he gave his life in propagating knowledge wherever he found the opportunity.
>
> You know much better than I do how great those opportunities were and what wonderful use he made of them.........As we look back we shall think of his as a very wonderful, useful, and valuable life."

The Journal, Friday October 22nd.,1926

His son Horace and daughter Olive laid a floral tribute of flowers in the form of an open book with the inscription:

"His life is written in a book of flowers"

So what remains? His cottage in Martley was swept away many years ago; his house at 124, Embleton Road, Lewisham suffered the indignity of being demolished by bombing in the Second World War. His books, magazines, journals, and articles are all but gone. His first garden at "The Firs" has all but disappeared as well, swallowed up by the expansion of Lewisham, with only one or two local roads following the outline of the estate, and the last western section, a lake and surrounds, converted into a restored public park.

But one last story remains. In 1887 Common Land at Halstead in Essex was set aside to become a Public Park to celebrate Queen Victoria's Diamond Jubilee. However, before the project got off the ground (so to speak), local residents and ratepayers started to question the cost of laying out and maintaining the park at one half penny on their rates, Queen or no Queen Victoria.

Eventually they held a referendum - a singularly democratic way to make up their minds - and voted 474 to 359 in favour of carrying on with the project. Sanders was brought in to advise on the planting. A local industrialist, George Coulthard, pitched in with £1,000 to give the fund a flying start. But they did not get round to working on the park until 1899, and finished it in 1901, six months after Queen Victoria had died! So much for "Jubilee Gardens"

The Park had been designed "to ameliorate the lives of the Poor". It had a bandstand, a dancing green, a small lake, a children's playground, and a boundary ha-ha, which Sanders suggested could be filled with ornamental plants.

The lake was designed with a cascade. It was never constructed. Instead, a sort of rough rockery was built at the end of the lake using chunks of industrial stone left over from other developments - not a pretty sight, but presumably saving money for the careful folk of Halstead. Later on they added a war memorial.

£60 was set aside for 1,300 deciduous and evergreen trees and shrubs. In the marginal notes Sanders advised them to plant hollies to surround the park. Other plants he mentioned were snowdrops, scilla, rhododendrons (which apparently died), and rose bowers and arches (which seem to have been "Crimson Rambler" - a vigorous, easily maintained rose, resistant to disease). His notes also showed where to place the flower borders around the foot of specimen trees and shrubs to create a natural effect.

In time the park lost its railings for the war effort; the boundary, ornamental or otherwise, disappeared.

And then in 1999, a century since the original, a decision was taken to restore the park for the Millennium............and Sanders' "The Flower Garden" was used as a practical guide......

SELECTED INTRODUCTIONS AND FOREWORDS

THE AMATEUR'S GREENHOUSE (1904)

The term "greenhouse" appears to have originated from the occasional use in the seventeenth century of buildings with large windows in front for sheltering myrtles, orange trees, bay trees, and other more or less tender evergreen trees and shrubs during the winter months. Such trees were grown in tubs, and were placed outdoors during the summer months. The greenhouse of those early days consisted of a lofty building with a tiled roof, a brick wall at the back, similar ones at the ends, and glazed windows extending from the floor to the eaves of the roof. Sometimes the sashes or windows were separated by slender or substantial pillars. The first house of this kind was said to have been erected at Heidelburg, in Germany, in 1619.

So far as we can gather, the first greenhouse built in this country was in the early part of the seventeenth century, in the Apothecaries' Garden at Chelsea. Philip Miller, in his "Gardeners' Dictionary", published in 1731, makes the following quaint remarks on the subject: "As of late Years there have been great Quantities of curious Exotick Plants introduced into the English Gardens, so the Number of Greenhouses or Conservatories has increased, and not only a greater Skill in the Management and Ordering of these Plants has increased therewith; but also a greater knowledge of the Structure and Contrivance of these Places, so as to render them both Useful and Ornamental, hath been acquired."

He then goes on to describe the design and method of construction. He says the depth of the building should not be less than 16 ft., the length of the windows equal to the depth, their width 4 to 6 ft., and the piers between constructed of stone or oak. The floor is recommended to be of marble, stone, or tiles, and raised 3 ft. above the ordinary ground level. The ceiling and the walls should, he says, be white-washed or painted white, so as to reflect the rays of light upon the plants. Shutters were also advised to be fixed inside, so that in severe weather they could be closed over the glass to keep out the frost.

About the same period various means of artificially heating such structures were tried. Some used charcoal fires for the purpose, but the poisonous gases evolved suffocated the gardeners who had to attend them, and so this method was soon discarded. Then a plan of heating by flues was tried, and this proved a great success. Flues, 10 in. wide and 2 ft. deep, were carried around the front and back of the structure under the floor. The fire-place was usually outside in a shed, and the smoke and fumes carried up a flue built into the wall. In other cases, flues were built into the walls with fire-places outside so as to heat the walls, the warmth from which would radiate and increase the temperature of the inside air.

In the eighteenth century very little improvement was effected in the construction of greenhouses. Towards the close they were made of wood and glass, the panes of the latter being very small. During that period there was a heavy duty on glass, and this impost naturally retarded its use on a large scale. It was not until the fourth decade of the last century that the duty on glass was abolished. As a matter of fact, the glass duty was repealed from April 5th., 1845, by Sir Robert Peel, and income-tax introduced by him to make up for the loss of revenue. From that time the construction of greenhouses went ahead rapidly. At first the structures were mostly lean-to, then three-quarter span-roof, and finally span-roof - the latter now being the most popular, as well as the most serviceable form for plant culture.

Concurrently with the advances made in greenhouse construction during the latter half of the last century, so were great improvements made in the methods of heating them. Heating by steam supplanted the flue methods for a time. This, however, did not prove a safe or satisfactory plan. Then followed the low pressure system of heating by hot water in pipes, a method now brought to perfection, and in universal use. Then, as demand for small greenhouses increased, so did a similar need for small apparatus arise, and the introduction of hot air and hot water apparatus heated by oil and gas became an established fact.

Thus, in the words of Cowper:

> "Who loves a garden,
> Loves a greenhouse, too"

T.W.S.

("The Amateur's Greenhouse" was first published in 1904, and was reprinted in the following years - 1904, 1907, (1911), 1917, 1919, 1922. The British Library has the first, sixth, and seventh editions; Martley has the second, third, fifth, and seventh editions.)

BULBS AND THEIR CULTIVATION (1908)

Among the great wealth of vegetation at the command of man for decorating his garden and greenhouse few plants possess greater attractiveness, charm, or beauty than those that belong to the bulbous and tuberous-rooted section of the vegetable kingdom. Many of them have grace our gardens for centuries, been idolised and almost worshipped by our forbears, and in more recent times held in the highest esteem by flower lovers of every degree and in every station of life. Owners of princely demesnes have of late years adopted the commendable and artistic habit fashion of growing hardy kinds by the thousand in meads and woodlands; those of suburban and town gardens have also taken a supreme delight in cultivating them in beds, borders, and greenhouses; and others, again, who lacked the luxury of a garden, have shown an interest in these beautiful flowers by growing them on window-sill, the balcony, roof garden, and in the home. Still more interesting is the fact of children being encouraged to cultivate bulbs in pots, glasses, and bowls as a means of inculcating a love of nature, finding them a pleasant occupation for leisure moments, and developing the natural instincts of love, work, and delight within the minds of the young. A praiseworthy example of this phase of gardening has been set by the educational authorities of Sheffield, who every year distribute many thousands of bulbs for children to grow, and afterwards exhibit for prizes at an annual show.

In all ages bulbs and bulb culture seems to have been held in popular esteem. Even the barbarous Turk in bygone days excelled in the culture of the Tulip and Ranunculus, and regarded the plants as priceless treasures. The Greeks and Romans, moreover, delighted in growing lilies and hyacinths; and, in later days, history shows that the Flemish and Dutch indulged in the cultivation and admiration of a host of bulbous and tuberous-rooted plants. In

Holland and in France, indeed, the rage for rearing and cultivating tulips was carried on to such a degree that it developed into a mania. History affirms that in the seventeenth century the craze for these bulbs was so great that as large a sum as £10,000,000 sterling was received in Haarlem and district for new or rare tulips. For a single bulb of a variety named Semper Augustus the price of 4,600 florins, together with a new carriage, harness, etc., was paid. In other instances a single bulb was sold for twelve acres of land, and another for securities of the value of £5,000. Failing to secure the price asked from any one person, lotteries were arranged, and bulbs disposed of in that way. The result was, as in the modern instance of the potato boom, wealthy folk who gambled in so wild a speculation were reduced to absolute beggary, and the Government compelled to suppress the mania. Fortunately, in England no such craze has arisen. Lovers of daffodils, however, who are possessed of wealth do not hesitate to pay high prices for novelties, especially the newer varieties of narcissi.

One of the great charms of bulbous and tuberous-rooted plants is the fact of their flowering mainly at a period of the year when there is a paucity of other flowering plants. As Thomson has so happily expressed in verse:

"Fair-handed Spring unbosoms ev'ry grace
Throws out the Snowdrop,and the Crocus first;
The Daisy, Primrose, Violet darkly blue.,
And Polyanthus of unnumbered dyes;
The yellow Wallflower, stained with iron brown;
And lavish Stock that scents the garden round;
From the soft wings of vernal breezes shed,
Anemone; Auriculas enriched
With shining meal o'er all their velvet leaves;
And full Ranunculus, of glowing red.
Then comes the Tulip race, where Beauty plays
Her idle freaks; from family diffused
To family, as flies the father dust,
The varied colours run; and while they break

On the charmed eye, th' exulting florist marks,
With secret pride, the wonder of his hand.
No gradual bloom is wanting; from the bud,
First-born of Spring, to Summer's musky whiles:
Nor Hyacinths, of purest virgin white,
Low-bent, and blushing inward: nor Jonquils,
Of potent fragrance; nor Narcissus fair,
As o'er the fabled mountain hanging still;
Nor broad carnations, nor gay spotted Pinks;
Nor showered from ev'ry bush, the Damask rose.
Infinite numbers, delicacies, smells,
With hues on hues expression cannot paint,
The breath of Nature, and her endless bloom."

And not only in spring, but in dreary autumn and wintry days, to say nothing of summer, we have in the great family of bulbs and tubers precious blossom to add colour and gaiety to our gardens, window-sills, etc. In winter, for example, the hardy cyclamens, winter aconites, snowdrops, and some of the irises grace the rockery or the lawn with chaste and simple beauty. In spring the gay crocus, squill, narcissi, star-flower, Glory of the Snow, many irises, tulips, hyacinth, bluebell, anemone, dog's tooth violet and grape hyacinth are a few of the many beautiful bulbs and flowers that will flood the mead, woodland, and garden with a plethora of precious richly-coloured blossom. And what shall we say of summer days, when lilies galore, Spanish and English irises, early gladioli, ixias, sparaxis, and a host of other beautiful kinds, including the stately Eremuri, shed their floral refulgence on the garden and fill the air with dreamy fragrance? And when russety autumn arrives there are the meadow saffrons, the autumn crocuses and cyclamen, the gorgeous gladioli, and so on, to vie with the richness of the dying autumnal tints

As in our gardens, so in our greenhouses, we have a wealth of really beautiful subjects to cheer us in autumn, winter, and spring; indeed, if it were not for the great variety of bulbs, and the easiness with which they lend themselves to being force into flower, our greenhouses and hot-houses would not be the bright and cheerful spots they are in autumn and winter days.

Bulbs, indeed, are indispensable members of the vegetable kingdom, and it is well that we have not only a large number of genera and species, but also, thanks to home and Dutch growers, such a wonderful number of pretty varieties to suit all conditions of growth and all tastes as regards form and colour. In the gladioli, narcissi, and cottage or May-flowering tulip families we have, indeed, a glorious wealth of colour, mostly the product of enterprising growers in England and Ireland. It is a great satisfaction to know that these families of plants can be grown with such signal success commercially in our own country, and that we have not to depend entirely of foreign supplies for them.

The Cottage or May-flowering tulips are bulbs of such exquisite loveliness that they deserve a place in every garden. They come into flower in May and June, and help to form a connecting link between the ordinary spring-flowering and the summer-blooming bulbs. We cannot too strongly impress upon our readers the inestimable value of these tulips for massing in the borders or naturalising in grass, and everyone should make a point of growing some, at least, of the varieties and species named elsewhere. We might also speak in equally glowing terms of praise about the glories of the many precious types and varieties of the Narcissi family.

Lastly, we would strongly counsel the reader to study the tabulated list of hardy bulbs, and note the many kinds there advised for culture on rockeries. If it stimulates him to grow them, and to carpet the surface with lowly alpine plants, he will indeed derive great pleasure from the pursuit. And, above all, if the reader will only cultivate hardy bulbs in his cold house he will derive far greater satisfaction from them than from ordinary plants, and add immensely to the pleasure and profit of that most ancient and inspiring of all pursuits - the art and craft of gardening.

T.W.S.

Malvern—
The Rocks, Madresfield Court.

ROSES AND THEIR CULTIVATION
(1908)

The rose seems to have been a cherished flower from time immemorial. In Holy Writ the prophet Isaiah says: "The wilderness and the solitary place shall be glad, and the desert shall rejoice and blossom as the rose," but it is doubtful if the rose he mentions is the true one. However, the rose has long flourished in the Holy Land and the East generally, and so it is more than probable that the rose of Holy Writ may be the true one. Anyway, the ancients were well acquainted with the beauties and subtle charms of the rose, since Herodotus, Aristotle, Theophrastus, Virgil, and Pliny refer to it. The latter, indeed, says that the warriors of his time crowned themselves with garlands of roses during their feasts, and also covered their food with the petals or sprinkled it with the fragrant oil thereof.

In more modern times the rose has also been held in high esteem as an emblem of joy and sadness. Thus young folks used to decorate themselves with garlands of roses, strew roses on the ground before the happy bridal pair; and, according to Camden, a writer in the fifteenth century, "there was in his day a classical custom observed, time out of mind, at Oakley, in Surrey, of planting a rose tree on the graves, especially of the young men and maidens who have just lost their lovers, so that this churchyard is full of them." Then, it has long been a custom in this country to use rose-water to wash the hands and refresh the face after a banquet.

In other ways, less romantic, the rose has come into prominence in this country. As everyone who has read English history knows, the red and the white rose were chosen as emblems by the opposing factions in the War of the Roses, made famous by the immortal bard, Shakespeare:

“ ....This brawl to-day
Grown to this faction, in the Temple Garden,
Shall send, between the red rose and the white,
A thousand souls to death and deadly night.

Since that memorable affair the rose, however, has been regarded more as the emblem of peace. For the last three hundred years, at least, it has gradually become a favourite flower for decorating the garden, the greenhouse, and the home. Now the possessor of the humble cottage garden, the villa garden, and of the larger garden of the manor and palace, cultivates the rose by the dozens, hundreds, and thousands, and cherishes its brilliant and dainty colours and delicious fragrance more than that of any other flower. So popular, indeed, has it become that it has been crowned unanimously as the “Queen of Flowers.”

As showing the remarkable increase of varieties cultivated during the last three hundred years, we may mention that in 1581 ten sorts were described, in 1620 nineteen varieties, in 1784 twenty-one, in 1797 forty-six. In 1829 a French grower published a catalogue of 2,562 varieties, and ten years later the number had advanced to thousands. The varieties named in the schedule at the end of this volume by no means represent the whole of those in cultivation here and on the Continent. Still, the list is a formidable one. What we have done is simply to include the names of those to be found in the catalogues of English growers, omitting an immense number of kinds enumerated in French and German lists.

During the last hundred years a large number of books dealing with rose-growing has been published. Few of them have, however, achieved a greater amount of popularity than the present one, the first edition of which appeared in 1889. Since then three further editions have been issued, and now the publishers are issuing this, the fifth, with all the details brought up to date, including all the new varieties introduced during 1908. We have endeavoured to crowd into the volume every detail likely to be of practical value to the amateur rosarian, and we think we can honestly claim that the work contains more information on roses and their cultivation than any other book of the kind.

> "Rose! thou are the sweetest flower
> That ever drank the amber shower;
> Rose! thou are the fondest child
> Of dimpled spring, the wood nymph wild!
> Even the gods, who walk the sky,
> Are amorous of thy scented sigh."

T.W.S.

("Roses and Their Cultivation" was first published in serial form in 'Amateur Gardening', then as "Cultivated Roses" by Piper, edited by T.W.Sanders in 1899. It appeared under Sanders' authorship in 1904 and was reprinted in the following years - (1905), (1906), (1907), 1908, (1909), (1910), 1912, 1913, 1915, (1917), 1920, (1924), 1931. The British Library has the first, ninth, tenth, twelfth, and fourteenth editions; Martley has the first, fifth, eighth, twelfth, and fourteenth editions.)

THE ENCYCLOPAEDIA OF GARDENING (1911)

INTRODUCTION

The art and craft of gardening is unquestionably the oldest of all human occupations. Holy Writ tells us that when the Great Architect of the universe created Adam, the progenitor of our race, He placed him in that delightful earthly paradise, the Garden of Eden, to dress and to keep it. We, therefore, who have adopted the noble profession as a means of existence have every reason to feel justly proud of belonging to so ancient and honourable a craft, while those who have adopted other professions, and who practise the art and craft as a recreative pursuit, cannot but share a similarly grateful appreciation of its virtues.

PRIMEVAL GARDENERS AND GARDENS

In the long vista of time that has passed since the first grand old gardener practised the art, first for pleasure, and afterwards as a means of subsistence, gardening has never failed to have a magic fascination for rich and poor of all ages. Noah, we are told, experienced delight in cultivating the vine; Jacob in growing the vine, fig, and almond; Solomon in making gardens, orchards, and vineyards; and the ancient Egyptians, Assyrians, Chinese, Greeks, and Romans, in the fashioning of gardens, or the cultivation of fruits and vegetables. In fact, throughout all ages and all time, the noble craft has ever been a popular and fascinating pursuit.

King Solomon must have been an enthusiastic amateur gardener, since he tells us in Ecclesiastes that, "I planted me vineyards: I made me gardens and orchards, and I planted trees in them of all kinds of fruits: I made me pools of water to water therewith the wood that bringeth forth trees." The gardens of that period were enclosed by walls or thick hedges to protect the crops from prowling beasts, and the crops grown therein were the vine, fig, pomegranate, walnut, almond, medlar, and quince; lettuce, endive, cucumbers, onions, leeks, garlic, and melons; and roses galore. In the hot, dry climate of Palestine watering was an indispensable operation, and hence reservoirs and conduits for irrigating the land had always to be provided.

In ancient Persia and Assyria gardens were fashioned and maintained on an elaborate style in the neighbourhood of all great cities. Not only were all the choicest of the native flora utilised in their adornment, but others obtained from far-off climes. The famous Hanging Gardens of Babylon were the wonder of the then civilised world. These consisted of no less than twenty plateaux, rising one above the other, and resting on walls 22ft. in thickness, and each planted with trees or other vegetation, kept in constant growth by artificial watering. In Egypt, too, gardens were elaborately fashioned, sculpture and masonry entering largely into their formation and decoration. In these they grew every kind of fruit, vegetables, and flowers, all of which had to be increasingly watered by irrigation from the Nile, or by the hand of the slave.

MEDIEVAL GARDENING

The Grecians also were famous gardeners. They seem to have taken special delight in having fine expanses of beautiful greensward, studded with statuary and pavilions, and furnished with shady groves. Fruit trees were lavishly cultivated, and lilies, narcissi, and roses grown in profusion in these gardens. The Romans, indeed, were keen gardeners, and grew many of the popular vegetables of the present day with great success.

Moreover, they fully understood the art of manuring and forcing, and may be said to have brought the arts of horticulture and agriculture to their highest perfection at that period of the world's history. In China, Mexico, and in India, too, gardening was a popular pastime with rich and poor long before the Christian era.

So far as our own country is concerned, there is little doubt that we owe the early introduction of horticulture, and its sister art agriculture, to the Romans. When they had finally subjugated the ancient Britons, and peace prevailed, history tells us that the Roman settlers planted vineyards and orchards of apples, pears, figs, mulberries, etc., as well as grew corn, not only for home use, but also for exportation. In the twelfth century it is recorded that vineyards flourished in the vale of Gloucester, apple orchards were plentiful in the fertile county of Worcester, market gardens existed at Fulham, and that gardens attached to homes of the baron, yeoman, and kind were fairly common throughout England. But these gardens were not of the neat and symmetrical order of those of the present day. They were simple patches or enclosures within walls, planted with fruits, vegetables, and herbs. The monks of the Middle Ages were great gardeners. Their superior education, peaceful calling, and general habits fitted them to undertake the culture of produce in the curtilage of their monasteries. Moreover, they were in the habit of travelling a great deal, and had the opportunity of securing new or improved forms of produce to cultivate in their gardens.

GENESIS OF ENGLISH GARDENING

It was in the reign of Edward III, that the art of gardening began to be seriously take in hand. Britons then began to lay out their gardens on a more ornamental plan than before, and to cultivate plants for use and medicine more extensively. The first book on gardening, entitled "De Yeonomia de Housbrandia," by Walter de Henley, appeared in the 16th.century, and others soon followed, including the quaint Thomas Tusser, who detailed the work of the garden and farm in pleasing rhyme. In Henry VIII's reign the gardens of Nonsuch and Hampton Court were laid out with regal splendour, and in Queen Bess's time the potato, tobacco, tea, and a number of other useful or ornamental plants and trees were introduced from foreign climes to enrich the gardens of the period. Evelyn, then a great writer and traveller, did a great deal to popularise and extend the art of gardening; and Gerard, the famous surgeon and botanist, published his esteemed Herbal, a work still highly valued at the present day. John Parkinson later on published his "Paradisi in sole Paradisus terestris," a valuable work, which gave great impetus to furthering the art of gardening at the time.

In the eighteenth century marvellous strides were made in the progress of gardening. People of wealth began to lay out gardens on a magnificent scale, form parks, and plant trees for ornament and use. Botanic gardens were formed at Chelsea, Cambridge, and Kew, and greenhouses glazed with glass and artificially heated were first brought into practical use at that period. The professional gardener of the 18th century was, however, woefully lacking in skill and intelligence. He could cultivate ordinary crops, but failed to possess the art or initiative ofd growing the choicer vegetables and fruit, hence these had to be imported from Holland and Flanders. Later, he seems to have improved, and to have been able to understand the art of securing early crops and ensuring successional supplies.

GARDENING IN THE LAST CENTURY

It was in the last century that gardening in all its phases made the most rapid strides, thanks to the efforts of such eminent experts as Thomas Andrew Knight, who did so much in the improvement of the varieties of our hardy fruits; John Claudius Loudon, in the designing and planting of gardens and in the publication of his remarkable Encyclopaedia of Gardening, and Trees and Shrubs, etc., both works showing a unique mental capacity and an amount of personal industry unequalled to the present time; Sir Joseph Paxton, the talented gardener and designer of the gardens of Chatsworth and the Crystal Palace; Charles Darwin, who rendered immeasurable service to botany and the improvement of plants by his researches and studies as to the origin of species; Dr.Lindler, who did so much for us in regard to plant physiology and botany; and Dr.Maxwell Masters, in regard to coniferae - all men of noble character, high ideals, and the widest scientific and practical attainments, who have, alas! gone to their well-earned rest, and left behind them records of greatness that will never die out as long as horticulture exists.

It would, indeed, be an impossible task to mention even a tithe of those, living or dead, who have, during the past century, done so much for the art of horticulture, either by pen or deed. The long period of peace which we have enjoyed, the more widely diffused education which has prevailed, the immense help which the plethora of societies has rendered, and the marvellous increase of literature on the subject, have all been conducive to extending a love of horticulture far and wide throughout the kingdom.

It may truly be said that there is hardly a house outside our congested cities that does not possess a garden, and even in towns where garden space does not exist, the love of gardening often stimulates the citizens to form a miniature garden on the roof, or to grow flowers on the window-sill. Commercially, too, gardening has made rapid strides during the last fifty years. Thousands of acres are devoted to growing produce for market, and hundreds of acres are covered with glass houses to force early crops to feed the ever-increasing population of this country. Commercial horticulture is, indeed, a great industry, and is likely to become still more so in years to come. The latest new phase of the industry - the intensive system of growing early crops in frames, as so successfully practised in France - is now being tried in this country, and if it should prove a practical and financial success, we shall in due course see this island converted into a colony of gardens.

TASTE IN GARDENING

As regards taste in gardening, a wonderful change has taken place in this respect during the last half century. Our own memories carry us back to forty years ago, and since that time we have witnessed a remarkable revolution, not only in the fashioning of gardens, but in the manner of planting, and the kinds of plants grown. For example, our earliest experience of flower gardening was the strictly geometrical in design, and the planting of beds in a similarly rigid fashion - known as carpet bedding. In those days, the flaring zonal, and the tricoloured, bronze, gold, and silver-leaved pelargonium, the gaudy yellow calceolaria, and pyrethrum, and the brilliant blue lobelia, were the favoured plants for bedding, and hardy herbaceous plants and annuals were regarded as but of secondary importance. Every young gardener in those days regarded a knowledge of geometry as one of the essential accomplishments of his training, and many an hour was spent in devising intricate designs of a mosaic character for planting the beds next season. Plants with beautiful or richly-coloured foliage were much in demand for filling in the designs, and no amount of labour and expense was incurred in endeavouring to produce elaborate and ornate designs in the way of carpet or mosaic bedding. This style soon satiated the palate of the wealthy, and then followed the even more costly rage of subtropical bedding, plants of noble stature, richly-coloured foliage, or exquisite blossoms from tropical climes, being used extensively for decorating the flower garden. Eventually an apostle of Nature came upon the scene, in the person of Mr.William Robinson, a true natural artist, who fully appreciated the simple beauty and effectiveness of the wealth of hardy plants, and who unceasingly for forty years at least has urged upon owners of gardens the desirability of fashioning their gardens in a simple manner and more with regard to making them suitable homes for hardy plants, than as examples of geometrical art. Slowly the idea has gained favour with owners of gardens, with the result that to-day the strictly formal, hideous, gaudy, and repulsive style of garden decorations of forty years ago has given way to the more natural, simple, and truly artistic manner of transforming our gardens into pictures of natural beauty - the veritable reflex of Nature as seen in woodland, mead, or ravine. Thus, to-day, we see hardy flowering shrubs used to good effect in combination with evergreens, so as to make our shrubberies pictures of artistic beauty; our woodlands in spring carpeted with charming vernal blooming bulbs; the fringes of the lawn dotted with bold masses of golden daffodils; and our borders not planted with lines of gaudy geraniums, calceolarias, and lobelias as of yore, but with bold groups of hardy plants, that yield a continued succession of blossom from early spring to late autumn.

With the wealth of hardy trees, shrubs, plants and bulbs now at our disposal, it is indeed possible to have a garden beautiful in all its parts. We have kinds that revel in complete shade, in partial shade, and in full sun. The temperate regions of the world have, through the agency of the trade and travellers, furnished us with a remarkable wealth of vegetation for all our requirements, whether it be to plant a shrubbery, a rockery, a ravine, a dell, a border, or to clothe the walls of our dwellings. Thanks to the enterprise of our trade growers, it matters not what we require, we can get it, be it cheap or costly; every owner of a garden, indeed, has ample material to gratify his taste or meet the resources of his income.

GARDENING LITERATURE

As the love of gardening and the desire to become proficient in the knowledge thereof has increased, so has the demand for literature dealing therewith been more in request. Forty years ago the number of periodicals specially devoted to the art were few, about four weeklies then catering for the requirements of the enthusiastic gardener, while now there are about ten. In addition to these special journals, nearly every weekly paper of any importance, to say nothing of the dailies, publish a gardening article, thus showing the immense interest taken in the delightful hobby. Then during the last few decades hundreds, if not thousands, of books have been issued from the press, many dealing with the lighter side of gardening, and others of the more practical order. Every flower, every vegetable, and every fruit of any importance has formed the theme of a special monograph, while general subjects, as the greenhouse, flower garden, wild garden, woodland, fruit, etc., have also been dealt with in special volumes. The fact is, in later decades, owners have not been content to leave the "well ordering of their gardens" entirely to the professional gardener, but have developed the fashion of exercising the superior taste and scientific knowledge, the outcome of a good education, in the designing, planting, and general decoration of their gardens. This new departure has caused a wider interest to be taken in the art, and a general desire for literature of a pleasing as well as an educational nature. Thus publishers and authors have been stimulated to issue books to meet the demand for light and grave literature, with the result that the bookshelves of the enthusiastic amateur gardener literally groan beneath the ponderous weight of books on gardening.

A WORD ABOUT THIS VOLUME

Few books of the graver type have, perhaps, enjoyed such a wide circulation as the present volume. And why? The secret of its success is no doubt due to the fact that it conveys in a nutshell all that the busy man wishes to know about the cultivation of annuals, perennials, biennials, orchids, ferns, hot-house and green-house plants, climbers, bulbs, hardy trees and shrubs, water plants, fruits, and vegetables. It is a complete library in itself, and tells those who consult it in a very few words whether the plant or tree is hardy, half-hardy, or tender; what soil and what position it require; when to sow, plant, pot, or prune; and how it should be propagated. Such information has secured for the volume a popular reception, necessitating the issue of twelve previous editions.

When we first contemplated the idea of preparing the work we had no notion that it would command such a large sale. Really, we prepared the text more to publish as useful information for the readers of "Amateur Gardening" than as a separate volume, and did not take the same precautions to see that every subject was presented in alphabetical sequence, or as fully as we should otherwise have done. However, a strong request was made by readers for the publication of the text in volume form, and we acceded to it, not without misgivings that it was as perfect as we could wish. Edition after edition being called for, the necessity eventually arose for the entire work to be reset in new type, and then, with the full concurrence of the publishers, we decided to undertake the laborious task of thoroughly revising the details and nomenclature, and remedying the one weak point in the volume, namely, adding lists of the species belonging to each genus.

This work we have happily finished, and we are sufficiently self-conscious to believe that the work in its present form will be considered as perfect as human foresight, diligence, and care could possibly expect. We do not go so far as to say it is absolutely free from error. Anyone who has had any experience in the compilation of a dictionary - and there are very few, indeed, who have - knows full well the immense difficulties that have to be encountered in collecting and arranging the data, and in the subsequent reading of the proofs. Still, the task has been a pleasant one, as the Author knows from past experience that his efforts will be appreciated heartily by thousands of enthusiastic gardeners, not only in Great Britain, but beyond the seas.

It will be well, perhaps, to give a general idea of the improvements that have been made in the present volume. First of all, we have broken up the somewhat solid nature of the text which existed in previous editions by dividing the subjects into several paragraphs, so as to make each cultural feature distinct. Secondly, we have added considerably to the cultural data, giving, in the case of vegetables and fruit, more especially, the main points about the market culture of these crops. Thirdly, we have added the species and hybrids in general cultivation with their respective colours, time of flowering, height, and native countries, these being classified as hardy, half-hardy, annuals, biennials, perennials, trees and shrubs, green-house or hot-house plants, so that the reader may perceive at a glance the sections under which a species is classified. Fourthly, we have thoroughly revised the nomenclature of the genera, so as to bring them up-to-date. Thus, modern botanists now class the azaleas with the rhododendrons, the godetias with the oenotheras, the rhodanthes with the helipterums, and so on. This arrangement we have followed, so far as placing the species and cultural details are concerned. By means of cross references, however, we have placed the old familiar names in their proper sequence, so that the reader can easily get a clue to the facts he requires. Fifthly, cultural details are given under the generic name only, as the apple and pear under Pyrus; the plum and cherry under Prunus; the cabbage, broccoli, etc., under Brassica; carrot under Daucus; auricula and polyanthus under Primula, and so on. Lastly, we have included in alphabetical order all the common names in general use.

As regards the genera included in the present volume, they are those in general cultivation in gardens. Those only of botanical interest, or little grown, are excluded, because we are desirous, in conjunction with the publishes, that the volume shall be issued at a price within the means of all classes of amateur gardeners.

It has been suggested by many readers that we should give the pronunciation of the generic and specific names included in the work. We certainly did entertain the idea, but eventually found the task an insuperable one. Authorities vary so much in their ideas as to the correct pronunciation, that had we attempted the task, even with the aid of a good friend and classical scholar, we should have laid ourselves open to severe criticism. Besides, the expense involved in setting up the accentuations would have prevented the work being issues at a popular price.

A LAST WORD TO THE READER

Now we close this introduction, embracing a brief, general survey of the progress of gardening from the earliest to the present period, and of the general features of the volume, with a sincere hope that the busy man, who requires a fund of information in a small compass, will find this work - the reflex of forty years' practical and scientific study and experience, including twenty-three years' special acquaintance with the needs of amateur gardeners as Editor of "Amateur gardening" - a real friend, guide, and counsellor in all that appertains to the culture of vegetation in the garden and greenhouse.

T.W.S.

("The Encyclopaedia of Gardening" was first published in 1895, and was reprinted in 1896, 1897, 1899, 1900, (1901), (1902), 1904, (1905), (1906), 1907, (1908), (1909), 1909, 1911, 1913, 1918, 1919, 1922, 1926, (1928), 1930, 1931, and 1932. At least another thirty seven impressions are recorded up to 1972 and beyond. The British Library has the second, second revised, tenth, thirteenth, sixteenth, seventeenth, eighteenth, nineteenth, twenty-first, and twenty-second editions; Martley has the third, fourth, seventh, fourteenth, fifteenth, sixteenth, seventeenth, nineteenth, twenty-first, twenty-second, and twenty third editions.)

LAWNS AND GREENS
(1920)

One of the chief charms of a well-ordered garden is its velvety green turf. As a famous garden artist has so aptly expressed: "The lawn is the heart of the true British garden." In no other country is this delightful feature of the garden seen in such perfection in normal times as in this sea-girt isle. Every owner of a garden prides himself upon the possession of a good lawn, and well may he do so, for there is nothing forms so exquisite a setting to a floral picture as an expanse of emerald-green grass, and no costly carpet can ever vie with the springiness or elasticity of well-kept turf

Granted that the lawn forms so essential a feature of the flower garden, it naturally follows that every owner of a garden wants to know the correct methods of forming a lawn, and also of its subsequent management. To meet these requirements the present handbook was published some years ago, and it met with such appreciation from the public that two editions of it have been exhausted, and a third one is now presented to meet a further continued demand for copies.

This work, by the way, is not solely confined to the theme of the lawn alone; it covers a much wider field than that, and caters for the requirements of lovers of such manly and healthy sports as bowls, golf, cricket, tennis, etc. It contains full details on the formation and management of bowling greens, golf links, cricket pitches, and tennis and croquet lawns, and, therefore, may be said to be a complete vade mecum on all that pertains to the subject of greensward for beauty, pleasure, or sport.

No pains have been spared to render the present edition as accurate and widely useful in its contents as a long experience, wide observation, and human foresight would allow. In its pages every phase of formation and management is clearly dealt with, and a full description of weeds and their eradication, feeding and top-dressing, mowing machines, rollers, tools, and appliances, with advice as to their uses given, so that the reader can readily solve any problem concerning lawns, bowling greens, golf courses, or cricket pitches that may arise from time to time.

We have also endeavoured to illustrate the work by diagrams, sketches, and photographic reproductions, and thus, we hope, added to its usefulness, as well as its attractiveness.

Lastly, we desire to point out that the prices quoted in the following pages for seeds, turf, labour, etc., are approximate. owing to the unsettled conditions of labour and prices of materials, it is impossible to give an accurate estimate of cost. Hence the reader will, we trust, bear these facts in mind when considering the cost of laying lawns and greens.

1920 T.W.S.

("Lawns and Greens" was first published in 1911, and again in (1917) and 1920. The British Library has the first and third editions; Martley has the third edition)

VEGETABLES AND THEIR CULTIVATION (1920)

The cultivation of vegetables is, next to that of fruit, one of the oldest phases of the gardening art and craft. The reader has only to refer to the brief historical sketch given in connection with each of the numerous vegetables described in the following pages, to verify this statement. He will find there that many of the vegetables which are still extensively grown in British gardens, were known to, and grown by, the ancient Egyptians, Romans, and Greeks, to a very large extent, as articles of food and physic.

The ancient Romans were certainly adepts in vegetable culture, not only in season, but also out of season, since they well understood the art of forcing, for it is recorded that the Emperor Tiberius had cucumbers produced by artificial heat. To the Romans, no doubt, we owe, in a large measure, the introduction, after their conquest of Britain, of many vegetables and methods of cultivation which formed the foundation of our modern practice.

Concurrently with the introduction of Christianity, and the establishment of monasteries, fruit and vegetable cultivation began in earnest. The monks were keen gardeners, and doubtless grew both vegetables and fruit extensively and successfully. The first record we have of any published work referring to vegetables, appears in "Synopsis Herbaria," written by one Henry Calcoensis, a prior of the Benedictine Order. This worthy travelled extensively on the Continent to observe and glean what information he could on vegetables and their culture. The date of this work is A.D.1493. In another work, entitled "Arnolde's Chronicle," published in 1521, the author professes to tell his readers how to rear a salad in an hour.

It is, however, to Thomas Tusser, the author of the "Five Hundred Points of Good Husbandry," published in 1561, that we owe the opportunity of an insight into the kinds of vegetables grown in England in earlier days. Many of his quaint references are reproduced further on in the book.

Later in the century, John Gerard, or Gerarde, published his famous "Herbal," which contains elaborate references to herbs used as food and medicine. Then, in 1629, appeared Parkinson's "Paradisi in sole Paradisus terestris," a reprint of which delightful work has recently been published by Messrs.Methuen & Co. Under the title of "The Ordering of the Kitchen Garden," he gives many quaint instructions on the proper cultivation in his day, of vegetables and herbs.

The first work solely devoted to vegetable culture was, so far as we can verify, "The Practical Kitchen Gardener," by Switzer, published in 1727. Here full details how to lay out a kitchen garden, grow vegetables outdoors and on hotbeds are given. From then onwards many books and pamphlets have been written, down to the present day.

So much by the way. We have briefly sketched the progress of literature devoted to vegetables and their cultivation up to the present day. It is our business now to justify our reasons for placing another volume on the subject in the market.

There are, we admit, many excellent books on vegetable culture in existence, but, to our mind, they all fall short of fulness of information on all branches of the subject. Having had to cater for the requirements of amateur gardeners for over thirty-one years, and being, therefore, cognizant of their requirements; also, in addition, having had a long practical experience as a gardener, and consequently well acquainted with the needs of the professional gardener - especially the probationer - we came to the conclusion that an up-to-date work, written in simple language, and giving a very wide range of information, was badly needed - hence the present volume.

In preparing the work we have endeavoured to cater for all requirements, and especially to give such information as would be useful and interesting to the student, as well as to the practical grower. Thus, we have given the botanical name and family of each vegetable, its foreign names, and a brief resume of its history.

Then, in the practical departments, we have dealt fully with laying out a vegetable garden; cropping; general management; pests and diseases; soils and manures; friends of the gardener; and finally have described with sufficient fulness the culture of herbs and vegetables generally grown in British gardens.

Finally, we hope the student, the probationer, and professional gardener, as well as the amateur gardener and the allotment holder, will find the volume as useful and as interesting to him as the heavy labour involved in its preparation has been a pleasure and a work of live to ourselves.

Although every care has been bestowed on its preparation, and in passing it through the press, a few errors may have unavoidably crept in. but, in the event of any being discovered, we shall only be too grateful to the reader if he will point them out.

1920 T.W.S.

("Vegetables and Their Cultivation" was first published in 1905, and then in (1907), (1911), 1917, 1919, 1920, 1928. The British Library has the first, fourth, fifth, and seventh editions; Martley has the sixth and seventh)

THE FLOWER GARDEN (1921)

THE GARDEN BEAUTIFUL

Throughout the whole world it would be difficult to find a fairer or more beautiful spot than a properly fashioned English flower garden. Its lovely green lawn, the envy of all visitors to these shores; its wealth of beautiful trees and shrubs, and its array of charming hardy flowers, tastefully and artistically disposed in happy unison with each other, constitute a picture of supreme loveliness almost beyond the power of language to adequately describe.

We may, it is true, in other lands, see gardens fashioned in a more elaborate style, such as Italy and France for example, but the excessive use of architectural and sculptural features so utterly overwhelm the arboreal and floral ones that they appear wanting in that simple, natural beauty which is so strong and marked a characteristic of the genuine English garden. In years gone by many of the larger gardens in this country were fashioned on similar lines, and the compare very poorly indeed in beauty and interest with latter-day examples in which nature and true art have had a strong influence in the designing and planting thereof.

And not only in large gardens, but in the smaller type of town and suburban gardens also there existed a similar taste in design and adornment. Fancifully constructed grottoes, a plethora of wire or iron arches, rustic margined beds, vases galore, and the inevitable rockery of plain or coloured glass, etc., were all regarded in the earlier part of the last century as indispensable features of a well-designed garden. Even in the country cottage garden precious hours and days were spent in clipping and trimming the sombre yew tree into some fantastic shape, such as a peacock, a dog, or a goblet. The idea of rigid formality, like the germ of a disease, spread throughout the length and breadth of the land, making gardens more or less hideous by such ugly features.

And in gardens generally, we well remember in the days of our youth, over forty years ago, how the many lovely and interesting hardy flowers which are so thoroughly esteemed to-day, were regarded as mere weeds, only worthy of a place in out of the way corners. In those days the flaming zonal pelargonium, the gaudy calceolaria, the brilliant blue lobelia and so on were regarded as the only plants worth using for the summer decoration of the garden. Hence what would otherwise have been beautiful expanses of lovely greensward were cut up into geometrical beds, and borders were formed everywhere as fringes to the shrubbery or otherwise to accommodate the endless rows of these flaming flowers. When such borders formed the fringe of a shrubbery, the shrubs were of secondary importance, and so the shoots thereof were rigidly cut back to form a dense wall of greenery, regardless of any special beauty each shrub possessed. The carpet bedding mania came into vogue about the same time. The idea caught on with professional gardeners of all grades, and no garden was considered complete as regards its summer bedding without one or more of the fancifully designed flower patterns. The more intricate the design the more the pattern was admired, consequently the demand for originality in design was so great that gardeners spent many sleepless nights in trying to evolve something new from their brain. Then came the necessity also for securing suitable plants, the time and great expense in growing them, and after-labour and cost in planting and keeping the plants trimmed in regularly to maintain the features of the design.

Happily, such features as we have just enumerated are giving way slowly to a more rational and beautiful style of fashioning a garden. Owners of gardens are less inclined than formerly to entrust the fashioning of their gardens to the professional or landscape gardener, or the nurseryman or jobbing gardener. People, now-a-days, prefer the garden beautiful to the stereotyped, humdrum, formal garden of days gone by. They prefer to fashion their gardens in a simple and natural manner, and to make the tasteful and artistic grouping of the vast wealth of hardy trees and shrubs and plants the chief feature, design being of secondary importance.

There is no doubt that the great secret of ensuring the garden beautiful is to study primarily the question of finding a suitable home for the various classes of hardy plants. Thus, if a speciality is to be made of alpines, of bog plants, of aquatics, of roses, of ferns, of hardy trees and shrubs, and so on, the gardener must, in fashioning the garden beautiful, first select the best sites for these, and then assimilate the general design of the whole to suit the requirements of the former. No garden can be made really beautiful from a fixed design drawn beforehand. It is true a rough idea may be prepared for general guidance, but the best way to go to work is to set out on the plot the sites for the more important classes of plants it is desired to grow, and then adapt the remaining proportion of the garden accordingly.

The primary features of the ideal garden beautiful, as fashioned to-day are, first of all, a good expanse of lawn cut up with as few beds as possible. A lawn always makes a fine feature in an English garden. Secondly, plenty of border space should be provided to grow hardy flowers and bulbs. Thirdly, ample space should be provided also for trees and shrubs, more especially those that flower. Fourthly, paths or walks should be as few as is consistent with actual requirements for gaining access to important parts of the garden. In gardens of the larger type grass walks are preferable to gravel paths in many parts thereof. In small gardens it is a mistake to waste so much valuable space in having paths all round the garden. A path up one side is sufficient, the rest being turf and border. Fig 1 shows the usual plan of laying out a suburban garden, with a border of narrow width, and paths all round - the wrong way to lay out a garden. Fig.2 shows a similar plot with ample border space on the south or sunny side, and only one path. The dark shaded portions are the borders. In a garden thus fashioned there is ample room to grow flowers successfully. At T. (Fig.2) flowering trees may be planted to give shade and beauty. At the west end a summer house and rockery are shown, the whole being a more pleasing arrangement than the stereotyped design depicted in Fig.1.

Features to avoid in garden fashioning are: using wire arches too freely; placing the formal ready-made summer house in too prominent a position; placing too many vases about; fixing stone fountains in the middle of a lawn; using tile edgings too freely, and generally making the garden too trim and neat.

Now-a-days, true garden lovers strive to fashion their gardens after some of the many charming examples to be met in some of our English landscapes. Thus the lawn is carpeted here and there in bold masses of daffodils or snowdrops in spring; shady banks clothed with coloured and yellow primroses; hedge banks and woodlands or shrubberies decorated with bluebells; shady nooks and corners made beautiful and interesting with ferns; ugly trees beautified by the rambling shoots of clematises or roses wreathed in blossom; the conformation of the surface broken up by pleasing undulations and planted with groups of pretty trees and shrubs, so as to form charming grassy glades and pretty spots to wander in, and so on.

The chief point to bear in mind in fashioning gardens is to make them as beautiful as possible. This can only be done by studying Nature's ways and relying as little as possible upon the skill of the geometrician. After all a garden is, or should be, a home for cultivated vegetation, and each plant, or tree, or shrub should have its requirements studied so that it can yield its natural beauties to the most pleasing effect. We use rustic or

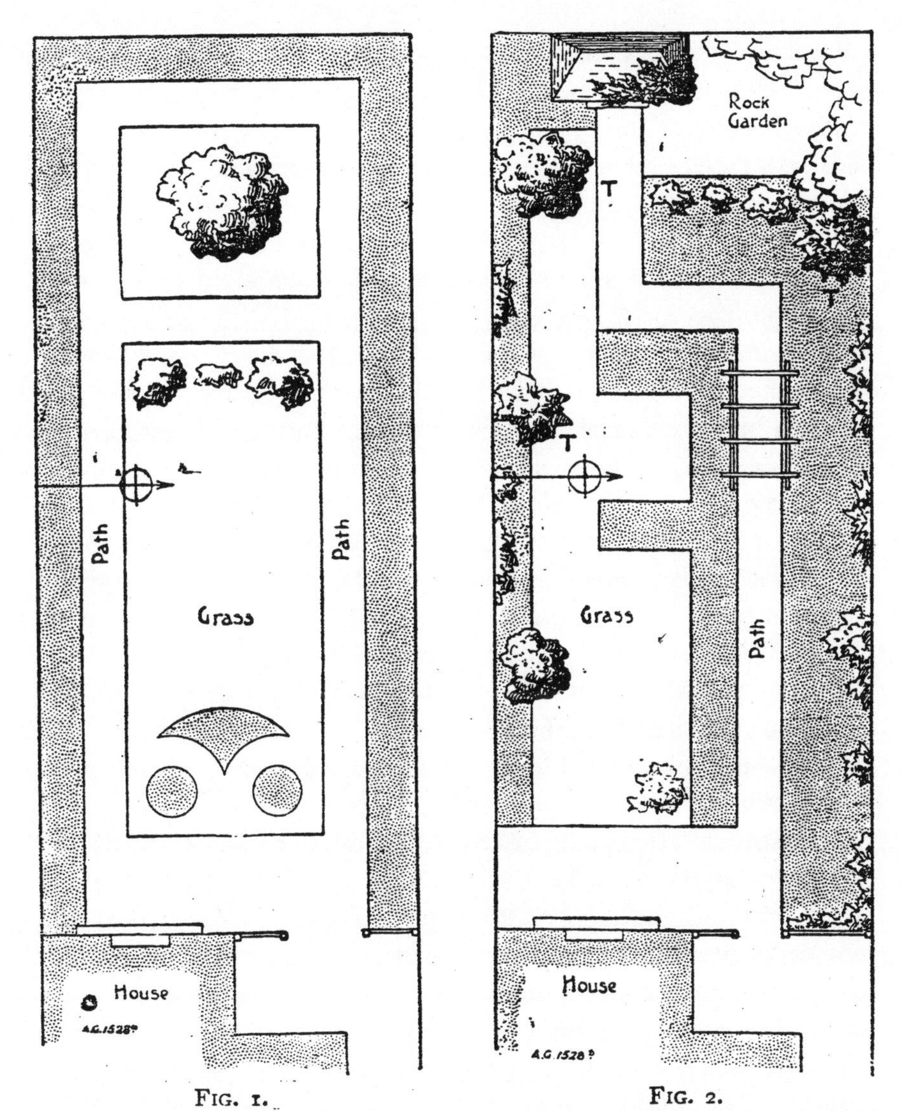

FIG. 1. FIG. 2.

EXPLANATION.—Fig. 1 shows the wrong way to lay out a garden, and Fig. 2 the correct way to do it.

wire arches in our gardens not for the sake of any beauty they may possess, but as a means of supporting climbers, the beauty of which we do admire; and so it is not the shape or number of beds, or paths, we may have in our gardens that yield any interest or charm, but the plants we cultivate.

In large or small gardens the importance of growing beautiful flowering trees and shrubs should not be overlooked. Far too many common kinds are grown in gardens. If the reader will only attentively read the sections devoted to hardy trees and shrubs, he will find a great variety of charming kinds that are a hundredfold more beautiful than common laurels, privets, and the general run of trees and shrubs grown in many gardens. Nor should the value of the wealth of hardy creepers and climbers for clothing bare walls and fences and ugly objects be overlooked. There are plants, trees, shrubs, and climbers to suit every position in the garden, whether it be in sun or shade, described in the various sections further on in this volume.

Finally, as the late George H.Ellwanger, the author of that charming American volume "The Garden's Story," truly says: "No arbitrary rules will suffice to make a garden, for, in the very nature of things, no two gardens can be just alike. Each one should seek his own expression in the combination he strives for. For this there exists infinite variety of material, adaptable to the particular soil, exposure and character of the space one would adorn and idealize. A charming feature of one garden may not be attainable in another, either through lack of space, difference of exposition, or natural incongruity. Thus, a miniature pond for the cultivation of bog plants - a delightful feature of the garden where it may be carried out - cannot be introduced with propriety on high exposures. Nor can a bank of ferns be placed to advantage where they have not the coolness and shade with which they are associated, and without which they cannot be satisfactorily grown." Furthermore, remarks the same author, "The great secret of successful gardening is continuity of bloom - a luxuriance of blossom from early spring to late autumn; so that, when one species has flowered, there will at once be something else to continue the blossoming period without leaving unsightly gaps of bare ground. Plant permanently, mass boldly. Do not confine yourself to a few kinds when there is such a wealth to choose form - plants for sunshine and plants for shade, plants for colour and plants for fragrance, plants for spring and plants for autumn, plants for flower and plants for form. Aim at individuality, to produce an ideal of your own."

Reader, you have in Mr.Ellwanger's words the fashioning of the garden beautiful in a nutshell. Read, mark, learn, and digest the contents of the succeeding pages, and if you fail to produce a beautiful and interesting flower garden it will be more or less your own fault.

T.W.S.

("The Flower Garden" was first published in 1907, and then again in 1915, 1919, 1921, 1925, and in revised form in 1935. The British Library has all six editions, Martley has all but the third.)

ANNUAL FLOWERS
(1924)

The present work is intended as a companion volume to the Author's previously-published book on "Popular Hardy Perennials," which dealt exhaustively with the culture and propagation of the various genera, species and varieties of hardy perennials for the decoration of the garden. Since hardy annuals and biennials are so closely associated with hardy perennials and because they possess the sterling merits of great attractiveness, as well as easiness of culture, and form a comparatively cheap method of stocking a garden, we came to the conclusion that a volume specially devoted to a description of the numerous kinds, with practical hints as to their uses and culture, would receive a hearty welcome from lovers of hardy plants.

Hardy annuals and biennials lend themselves to so many ways of beautification. They can be successfully grown in beds or borders, in pots on the window sill, or in the cold greenhouse, in verandahs or on the roof garden, in hanging baskets, on rockeries, as climbers, and so on, the wealth of genera, species, and varieties available for such purposes being of considerable magnitude. Moreover, they are quite as much at home in the town and suburban, as well as the country garden, and their inexpensiveness constitute them "everybody's flowers."

And the same eulogy may be fittingly applied to the great variety of half-hardy annuals. It is true they are not so easily produced as hardy annuals, because artificial heat is necessary to rear the seedlings successfully; but those who have the good fortune to possess a heated greenhouse, or can secure the materials for making a hotbed, can certainly command some really beautiful plants for the summer decoration of their garden or greenhouse. There are, indeed, few plants to surpass the charm and beauty of China Asters, Stocks, Phlox Drummondi, Salpiglossis, Nemesias, etc., for the summer beautification of beds and borders. Besides, many kinds are equally suitable for pot culture in the greenhouse, on the window sill, the roof garden, or in the verandah. A complete list of these, together with cultural details, will be found in the following pages.

Nor have we overlooked the value and charm of tender annuals for the adornment of the greenhouse in spring and summer. It is true we have included several genera which are not strictly of annual duration, because modern experience and practice have conclusively proved that they are capable of yielding better results when grown as such. Primulas, Cinerarias, and Calceolarias, for example, produce a much finer display of flowers of superior excellence and quality when treated as annuals.

Finally, we know, from thirty-seven years' experience as Editor of "Amateur Gardening," that the majority of amateur gardeners take a keen interest in the rearing of plants from seeds, and so we feel confident that they will extend a hearty welcome to this volume for affording them the needful guidance, not only as to what kinds in each section they can easily rear from seed, but, also, how to grow them successfully for the decoration of the garden or greenhouse. In the descriptive lists we have clearly pointed out which are true annuals, biennials, or perennials. In a sentence, the volume deals with plants that can be successfully grown as annuals or biennials.

T.W.S.

("Annual Flowers" was first published in 1924. Both the British Library and Martley have the edition, which was also reissued in a larger format)

THE ALPHABET OF GARDENING (1927)

"How shall I do it?"

This question always arises for the beginner when he or she is faced with the problem of the right way of digging his or her garden or plot, of the pruning of the rose tree, the planting of a bulb, the sowing of flower or vegetable seeds - and to his or her need is a simple, helpful answer.

Well, the "Alphabet of Gardening" supplies the want. If proof were needed of this it surely lies in the striking fact that such has been the popularity of the "Alphabet of Gardening" that this work has reached its eighth edition!

Not the least gratifying feature is the very large number of letters the Author has from time to time received from men and women readers who have found their gardening problems solved, or who have written to him as Editor of "Amateur Gardening," telling him of their successes in garden and plot cultivation.

There are some beginners who regard the spade and fork as the magic wand of horticulture, and think that all that is necessary is to attack the soil vigorously with their implements, push seeds, bulbs, or tubers into the ruffled earth - and then, hey presto! in the manner of the Indian Mango trick, the garden beautiful, or the plot bountiful, must appear, and when it doesn't they give up or blame the spade.

Spade-work is the primal secret of good gardening - but the spade needs to be used with knowledge, and it is not the thing that matters as the contents of this volume will show.

For the information of new readers it may be mentioned that this book was originally prepared as a primer for beginners in the art and craft of horticulture. Its purpose was, and still is, to teach the rudiments of the science and practice of plant physiology, the nature and treatment of soils, the office and uses of manures and fertilisers, the propagation, planting, sowing and cultivation of crops, and other gardening operations. A life-long experience has been drawn upon to give the why and wherefore of the scientific and practical phases of the art, and that technical knowledge is told as simply as possible. Successful cultivation depends upon the understanding of these vital facts.

This new edition has been thoroughly overhauled and enlarged. New diagrams have also been freely used to assist in illuminating and explaining the various scientific and practical facts described in the text, and every endeavour made to produce a really useful primer for the guidance of the garden novice.

The present work may indeed be regarded as an indispensable auxiliary or companion to the Author's popular "Encyclopaedia of Gardening," a book which has passed through eighteen editions, and deals in a concise manner with the cultivation and propagation of every genus and species of hardy and half-hardy tree and shrub, annual, biennial and perennial, hothouse and greenhouse plant, fruit, and vegetable suitable for growing in this country. It supplies the missing link - the elementary details of practice which are essential to guide the novice in the successful carrying out of the various operations there briefly given in connection with the culture and propagation of each genus. The possession, therefore, by an amateur or young professional gardener of the "Encyclopaedia of Gardening" and the "Alphabet of Gardening" provides him with a vast source of useful, practical, and scientific information "in a nutshell," so to speak.

The Author therefore hopes that the present volume will meet with the hearty appreciation of its readers, and that the information given therein will enable them to attain still greater success in the tilling and enriching of the soil, thus ensuring a more bountiful harvest of food crops, beautiful gardens, and gayer greenhouses in the future.

The true mission of the gardener should, indeed, be:

> "To study culture, and with artful toil
> To 'meliorate and tame the stubborn soil;
> To give dissimilar yet fruitful lands
> The grain, the herb, the plant that each demands;
> . . . . . .
> These, these are arts pursued without a crime
> That leave no stain upon the wings of Time."
> - Cowper

1926 T.W.S.

The publishers regret that since this Edition was revised for press Mr.T.W.Sanders has passed away. This revision was the last undertaken by him

February 1927

("The Alphabet of Gardening" was first published in 1907, and then in 1908, (1909), 1911, 1913, 1919, 1921, and 1927. The British Library has the first, fourth, sixth, seventh, and eighth editions; Martley has the second, fifth, and eighth.)

BIOGRAPHICAL RECORDS AND REMINISCENCES

VICAR'S HILL, LEWISHAM,

9904. 6/23.

LONDON, S.E.13 June 26th 192

Dear Mrs Fidoe,

I am indeed glad to hear the good news that the worries over the Show have disappeared & that it has been decided to hold an Exhibition this year on Aug. 25th. The latter date will suit me admirably as I shall be free to go & help you with the judging. My Assistant Editor will have returned by then from his holidays.

I enclose a list of books which I shall be pleased to place at your disposal to allocate as prizes to any classes you like.

Amateur Gardening: Editorial Office,
124, Embleton Road,
Lewisham SE15

March 7th.,1921

Dear Mr.& Mrs.Fidoe,

We were both very pleased to hear the good news that your son Hugo and Miss Somerton were able to get the cottage and enter into what we hope will prove a long and happy married life. I was especially pleased to hear that the Squire proved so amenable and gentlemanly at the prelimary *(sic)* party you gave. "All's well that ends well."

I have personally had a tough time for some weeks. The bitterly cold weather brought on a bronchial attack which clung resolutely to me until a week ago, but since the warmer weather set in, the "fiend" has vanished, not, I hope, to return this spring.

Mrs.S fortunately, has kept very well. We have both been talking about you & dear old Martley today & longing for the brighter weather to come, & with it the glorious spring flowers in hedge bank, in mead & in copse, so that we come & enjoy a sojourn with you. Easter, however, comes early this year, too early to enjoy the beauties of the countryside & so we must, I fear, postpone our visit to Whitsun. Anyway it would be too cold for Mrs.S., but if I can get free from my previous heavy literary toil of bringing out new editions of several of my books I may feel inclined to arrange for a few days at Easter. If you should be free to have me then I should like to visit the old place again, but pray don't upset any arrangements you have made on my account.

With kind regards to you all from both of us, believe me

Yours always sincerely

T.W.Sanders

Amateur Gardening: Editorial Office,
124, Embleton Road,
Lewisham SE15

June 26th.,1923

Dear Mrs.Fidoe,

I am indeed glad to hear the good news that the worries over the Show have disappeared & that it has been decided to hold an exhibition this year on Aug.25th. The latter date will suit me admirably as I shall be free to go & help you with the judging. My Assistant Editor will have returned by then from his holidays.

I enclose a list of books which I shall be pleased to place at your disposal to allocate as prizes to any classes you like.

I think the idea of having a separate Secretary for each section a good one. It will certainly work more smoothly & successfully than in the past.

Of course I should be only too delighted to have the assistance of my dear old friend John White in judging the exhibits. I think the pair of us can manage unless you know of anyone else.

Glad to say Bema *(?)* & I are keeping A.1. I believe she finishes at Somerset House in July & will then be home with me &, of course, she will be more free. Mr.Bartlett[1] often enquires about you; he thoroughly enjoyed the visit.

I am just off to the Royal Hort.Show at Westminster, & on Thursday to the National Rose Show, so have a busy week in store.

With all good wishes for the success of the show, and kind regards to all.

Yours always and sincerely,

T.W.Sanders

1. *Secretary, National Sweet Pea Society*

Amateur Gardening: Editorial Office,
124, Embleton Road
Lewisham SE15

April 15th., 192(6)

Dear Mrs.Fidoe,

Just a hurried line to say we are looking forward to seeing you on Thursday. We propose to travel by the 1.30 from Paddington, reaching Worcester at 3.40. Will you kindly arrange for Humpherson or Holliday to meet that train & run us out to Martley.

The weather has been attrocious *(sic)* here. East winds, sleet, snow, frost & rain have been a daily reoccurrence until today; it has been fine & warm so far. Olive has been very poorly, but is now better & is looking forward to seeing you. I am much better & I do hope the change will do us all good.

In haste

With kind regards

Yours always and sincerely

T.W.Sanders

Amateur Gardening: Editorial Office,
124, Embleton Road,
Lewisham SE15

July 28th.,1926

Dear Mrs.Fidoe

All being well I hope to be with you on Saturday Evening. I am leaving for Worcester by the 12.45, due at Worcester just before 3p.m. I am sorry Olive cannot accompany me, but she has a Devonshire friend who arranged to stay with her a long time ago & she cannot cancel the arrangements.

I have had a very anxious & arduous time to go through the last two months. So many of my books have run out of sale & I am busily engaged on bringing them up to date, which means much concentration of thought & hard work.

I shall try & catch the first bus out on my reaching the city.

With kind regards:

In haste

Yours always and sincerely

T.W.Sanders

PROCEEDINGS:
THE LINNEAN SOCIETY OF LONDON
(1926-1927 Page 95-96)

Although not particularly well known to botanists, T.W.Sanders was an outstanding figure in the horticultural world for nearly half-a-century.

. . . .

He was emphatic without being dogmatic, and his terse descriptions of plants and successful methods of cultivating them proved that above all else he was "a good practical gardener." But his descriptions were always pleasant reading, and thus made a greater appeal to amateurs than did the severely plain and practical observations of so many professional gardeners of that time. He had the genius to foresee the difficulties that amateur gardeners were likely to experience in their cultivation of flowers, fruits, and vegetables; he also possessed the knowledge of how best to avoid or overcome such difficulties.

. . . .

He established the National Amateur Gardeners' Association and was the driving force that made it an unqualified success; the meetings were crowded with enthusiasts who found in the President a man who resolved their difficulties without ridicule or the assumption of superior knowledge or intelligence.

. . . .

Sanders had an extraordinary capacity for work; he was unassuming, kindly, and considerate, and during the whole of his life he never failed to lend a helping hand to those in need of any assistance he was able to render.

C.H.Curtis

THE GARDENERS' CHRONICLE
(OCTOBER 23RD.,1926)

Sanders was a shining example of those who rise from the ranks by means of their own natural ability, coupled with persistent study and enthusiasm for their work.

. . . .

He had a whole-hearted belief in the educational value of travel, and whenever opportunities afforded, he visited continental countries for the purpose of studying horticulture and agriculture.

. . . .

Sanders while not claiming to belong to the old order of florists, had, nevertheless, a wide knowledge of floriculture and took great pain to encourage the raising and exhibition of new and improved varieties of all the popular garden flowers.

. . . .

As a lecturer, Sanders had a very happy manner, and was perhaps at his best when answering questions put by members of his audience.

. . . .

His patience and good humour stood him in good stead during all these years, and he was always ready to advise amateur gardeners concerning their difficulties in gardening, and no matter how insignificant or foolish a question might appear it was always answered in the kindliest fashion, as though the person immediately concerned was of the greatest possible importance in the horticultural world.

. . . .

Although his life was a long and very busy one, there is no doubt whatever that his good works will follow him and he will be kept in kindly memory for many years to come.

AMATEUR GARDENING
(OCTOBER 23RD.,1926)

It is with great sorrow of heart that we announce the death of Thomas William Sanders, F.L.S.,F.R.H.S., at the age of 71, after a brief illness.

By his death British horticulture has sustained a great loss, for it is unquestionable that he was a great and vital figure in the craft.

For nearly 40 years he edited Amateur Gardening, and, through the pages of this journal, and by his books, he has raised, so to speak, the great army of amateur gardeners as we know them to-day.

He exercised the most powerful influence in popular gardening of any writer of his day, and the secret of this lay largely in the fact that he had had unique practical experience of horticulture in all its branches, and of agriculture, too, combined with the natural skill of conveying it to others by his writing. Readers knew that they were getting sound advice in Amateur Gardening and in the books he wrote.

Besides his work as editor, Sanders was also known as the most distinguished horticultural author of his times. No other garden author has attained the sales that his books have, and will still have, for Sanders' "Encyclopaedia of Gardening" is a standard work, over a quarter of a million copies having been sold; so, too, are his "Fruit and Its Cultivation," "The Flower Garden," and so on. He wrote something like forty books, dealing with every phase of the art of gardening; they are a remarkable memorial of his love for gardens.

His industry was amazing. In addition to editing at one period two papers - Amateur Gardening and "Farm and Garden" - he found time to write books, deliver lectures (and his lectures, such as the "Garden Beautiful," always drew packed audiences), to attend horticultural gatherings, and personally often to advise people on their gardens. He early championed the allotment holders, and there are those of nearly 40 years ago who will still recall his relentless efforts on their behalf and in securing "little gardens" for the people.

It was often his custom to enter his study at 6.30a.m. and begin his day's work, and time has been when his green lamp would be gleaming in the early morning still.

As he had the gift of knowledge in regard to gardening, so he also had the gift of patience, and he was never too pressed to advise any who really sought to learn the art of making a small garden beautiful.

Deep in his heart he believed that if men and women made gardening one of their hobbies they would find peace and solace, and that a nation of gardeners - amateur gardeners - would not want to wage wars, except upon garden pests.

A heckler at a lecture once asked him "what flowers he liked best," and he answered that he liked them all, but the rose was the Queen of Flowers.

His letter-bag was extraordinary. Apart from his Amateur Gardening letters - and this meant many thousands of answers a year - he received letters from all over the world, from the African desert, where a lonely Englishman wanted to cultivate some home flowers; to South Sea Islands. Letters came from every walk of life, and peer and peasant received the same treatment from him.

Many tributes have been paid to him by those who read him, and he was proudest of that.

Amateur gardeners have lost a great friend in Sanders; it can truly be said that he lived for and loved his work.

VALDAR & SANDERS
MEMBERS OF THE INSTITUTE OF JOURNALISTS

PRINCIPALS:
LIONEL VALDAR
HORACE SANDERS

PUBLICITY CONSULTANTS
CHAPTER HOUSE · SALISBURY SQUARE
FLEET STREET E·C·4

TELEPHONE:
CENTRAL
5645

The Rev. James F. Hastings,
Rector of Martley.

Saturday,
July 29th.,
1 9 3 3.

Dear Sir,

I thank you for your letter and kind acceptance on behalf of the village of my father's portrait as well for the generous words in which you make reference to him.

It is the fact that he had a constant pride in being a son of Martley, and in many articles in a diversity of journals, he often wrote of Martley and the Teme valley. That a village should so impress itself upon the constant memory of one of its village boys is a tribute to the qualities of the village itself.

I will advise you as to the day on which the portrait is sent, which will be quite shortly.

Although I do not think I have ever had the pleasure of meeting you, my father often spoke of you to me, and in my young days I did have the pleasure of speaking several times to your venerable father who I remember very well indeed.

I shall certainly take occasion to visit Martley at an early date, and I shall be very glad to have the opportunity of meeting you.

Yours sincerely,

Horace Sanders

I hope in the meantime you will accept the latest revised edition of the Encyclopaedia.

GNC/JHS
24 September 1990

Editorial Department
Westover House, West Quay Road, Poole, Dorset BH15 1JG
Telephone: Poole (0202) 680586 Fax: (0202) 674335

Mr A L Boon
Old School House
Martley
Worcester
WR6 6QA

Dear Mr Boon

Thank you for your letter of 4 September and I apologise for the delay in replying.

I was interested to receive your letter and to know that you are conducting research into the life of T W Sanders. He was, in fact, the "Father" of Amateur Gardening. Apparently, he was a professional gardener who was appointed assistant editor by the first editor, Shirley Hibberd, in 1884. Hibberd, although a great authority, seemed to lack the common touch and only remained as editor for two years. Sanders took over as editor and reigned for 40 years - a remarkable achievement. He really set the magazine on the right path and on those foundations it has continued to flourish. It is interesting to know that he doubted his abilities to edit the magazine and only agreed initially to do the job for a year!! He died in 1926.

You may be interested to know that a former editor of the magazine, Arthur Hellyer, now approaching 90 but still a very active journalist, met Sanders in a hotel in Jersey in 1925. You might like to write to Arthur and he may be able to give you more information. His address is: Orchards, Rowfant, East Grinstead, Crawley, Sussex. You can tell him we have given you as much information as we have available.

When Sanders was editor, Amateur Gardening was owned by W H & L Collingridge, of Aldersgate Street, London. They also published the City Press, a financial newspaper, and a range of gardening books. Sanders wrote several but his outstanding achievement was "Sander's Encyclopedia of Gardening" which was published in 1895 and ran to 19 editions before 1931. After this it was enlarged and revised several times. We know of many gardeners who keep it beside them in the potting shed as it is so useful if you want to know quickly how to grow a particular plant.

continued

The rose "Sander's White" was not named after T W Sanders. The rose appeared in 1912 and came from Sanders rose nursery. We do not know of any other plants named after him.

We know very little about him before he came to Amateur Gardening and if you discover anything of interest we would like to have it for our files. Arthur Hellyer is now about the only person who could possibly have this information. We would be very interested to know where you saw the oil painting of Sanders. Who is the owner?

We still have a desk in the office which was presented to the magazine by the Sanders Family and there is a plate on the desk to this effect. It is interesting to see the desk surrounded by today's modern computers - a far cry from the days of Sanders when they did not even have female secretaries!

Yours sincerely

Graham Clarke
Editor

5th.,October, 1990

Dear Mr.Boon,

I did meet T.W.Sanders once, in May 1926 as far as I can remember, in the Chalet Hotel Jorfiere, Jersey where I was staying for a week with one of my aunts. He was with his invalid daughter and was pointed out to me as the editor of Amateur Gardening. I plucked up courage to ask him whether there was any prospect for a young man in horticultural journalism and he dashed any hopes I had by replying instantly "None whatsoever. I have an assistant who has been with me for about 30 years and when he dies I shall require one replacement." As it happened I was working in the Amateur Gardening Office by Jan.1929 and remained there until I retired in 1966, but that is another story.

This was the only time I met Sanders and your information about his birthplace and childhood is new to me. As I understand, when he left school he became a gardener and progressed to become a head gardener. When W.H. and L. Collingridge launched Amateur Gardening as a more popularly orientated weekly than any of the other gardening papers then being produced, they appointed Shirley Hibberd as editor and, for some reason unexplained, Hibberd engaged Sanders as assistant. After about a year, the management were dissatisfied with results and thought that Sanders might make a better job of meeting the needs of the kind of readership they had in mind. Apparently he was very uncertain of his ability to do this with so little journalistic experience but agreed to give it a trial for a year and stayed on until he died in 1926.

He was unusually successful both as editor of the paper and author of many books including the best selling "Sanders' Encyclopaedia of Gardening." This was finally absorbed into my own "The Collingridge Encyclopaedia of Gardening" in

1976 but I have to admit that this very much larger book, which included instruction about the work in gardens and the materials, methods, etc. involved (Sanders' encyclopaedia dealt with plants only) was nothing like the success of its much smaller, cheaper, more readily portable predecessor.

As far as I know Sanders, as editor, always lived and worked from Lewisham and had his editorial office in his own private house. H.A.Smith (I have just discovered, via the Lending Library that H.A. stood for Henry Augustus) lived nearby, walked round daily to work with Sanders and, once a week, visited the Collingridge office in London to bring copy and make up for the next issue and pass the pages of the current one. Smith and I worked for another 16 years or so before he finally retired.

Sanders played a very important role in the development of late 19th, early 20th century gardening, and this has never been adequately recognised.

Yours sincerely,

Arthur Hellyer

(Arthur Hellyer succeeded A.J.Macself as Editor of Amateur Gardening, and retired in 1966)

2001-01-29

KUNGL. MAJ:TS ORDEN

Mr David L Cropp
2, Vernon Close
Martley
Worcs WR6 6QX
England

Dear Mr Cropp,

In answer to your letter of January 14th this year to the chancery of the Royal Orders concerning Thomas W Sanders I can give you the following information.

As you tell in your letter Sanders was appointed Knight first class of the Royal order of Vasa, but in 1906 not in 1907. The circumstances were as follows:

On the 11th of July 1906 Hugo Lindgren, director of a whole-sale firm in Malmö dealing in dairy business and butter and cheese export, wrote to the Swedish ministry for foreign affairs a letter in which he among other things mentioned the following: "Last Monday (=9th of July) I had the honour to receive a number of distinguished representatives of the British agricultural press which in the last weeks have visited our country and studied our agricultural conditions." He goes on pointing out the importance of such a study tour for Swedish agricultural export and says that these Englishmen and Scots, experts in their field, worked mainly as chief-editors of the leading specialist newspapers precisely in those areas af Great Britain, northern England and eastern Scotland, where Swedish agriculture had their biggest, safest and most profitable market. The group had left Malmö very satisfied with their visit and had told their host of their decision to work for Swedish agricultural interests. He then continues suggesting that the minister for foreign affairs propose to H M the King that the leader of the group, Mr T W Sanders (124 Embleton Road, Ladywell, London) should be given a Swedish decoration. "Mr Sanders is an elderly man, of high esteem and greatly respected by his colleagues of the agricultural press. He is also a member of the Linnean Society in London, a fairly unusual and desirable distinction, that only is fitting for botanists of the first rank and men of integrity". Awarding him the order of Vasa should by the study group be regarded as a high Swedish honour and promote a still greater interest in Swedish agricultural products.

On the 19th of July the Ministry sent a copy of Mr Lindgren's letter to the Swedish envoy in London for his opinion. On the 7th of August the envoy, count Herman Wrangel, answered that it was important to stimulate the interest in Sweden and

KUNGL. SLOTTET S-111 30 STOCKHOLM TEL +46-(0)8 402 6000 FAX +46-(0)8 402 6005

especially in the export of Swedish agricultural products to Great Britain. He continues that Mr Sanders seems to have all the requirements to be of good use to Sweden and recommends him to be appointed Knight first class of the order of Vasa. (this corresondence in the archives of Ministry for Foreign affairs, 1902 års dossiesystem, vol 3565, National archives, Stockholm.)
On the 20th of October 1906 Thomas W Sanders was appointed (the register of the orders, Royal Palace, Stockholm) and on the 31st of October the badge of the order was sent to the Swedish legation in London.

Yours sincerely

Lars-Olof Skoglund
Archivist

ARTICLES, DOCUMENTS AND PUBLICATIONS

BOOKS WRITTEN BY T.W.SANDERS

( ) = assumed publication date

Allotments
1907 1st. edition
(1911) 2nd.

Allotment and Kitchen Gardens
1917 3rd.
1918 4th.
1919 5th.
(as **"Kitchen Garden and Allotment"**)
1925 6th.
1939 6th. revised

The Alphabet of Gardening
1907 1st. edition
1908 2nd.
(1909) 3rd.
1911 4th.
1913 5th.
1919 6th.
1921 7th.
1927 8th.
1927 8th. "mourning"

Amateur Gardening Month by Month
1920 1st. edition
1926 2nd

The Amateur's Greenhouse

1904 1st.edition
1904 2nd.
1907 3rd.
1910 4th.
1917 5th.
1919 6th.
1922 7th.

Annual Flowers

1924 1st.edition

Annuals

1904 1st.edition
1905 2nd.
1906 3rd.

Asparagus, Beans, Peas, Rhubarbs, Marrows

1904 1st.edition

Bulbs and Their Cultivation

1908 1st.edition
1913 2nd.
1923 3rd.

Carnations, Picotees and Pinks

1911 1st.edition

The Encyclopaedia of Gardening

1895	1st.edition
1896	2nd.
1897	2nd.revised
1899	3rd.
1900	4th.
(1901)	5th.
(1902)	6th.
1904	7th.
(1905)	8th.
(1906)	9th.
1907	10th.
(1908)	11th.
(1909)	12th.
1909	13th.
1911	14th.
1913	15th.
1918	16th.
1919	17th.
1922	18th.
1926	19th.
(1928)	20th.
1930	21st.
1931	22nd.
1952	23rd.

(at least thirty-seven impressions are recorded up to 1977)

Flower Foes

1923	1st.edition

The Flower Garden

1907 1st.edition
1915 2nd.
1919 3rd.
1921 4th.
1925 5th.
1940 6th.revised

Fruit and Its Cultivation

1915 1st.edition
1919 2nd.
1920 3rd.
1926 4th.
1940 5th.

Fruit Foes

1921 1st.edition

The Garden Calendar

1887 1st.edition

Garden Foes

1911 1st.edition

Garden Foes [combined]

1929 1st.edition a) blue boards/orange
b) green boards/white

Grapes, Peaches, and Melons [with J.Lansdell]

1924 1st.edition

Green Crops - Broccoli, Cabbage, Herbs

1904 1st.edition

Indoor Gardens

1913 1st.edition

Lawns and Greens

1910 1st.edition
(1911) 2nd.
1920 3rd.

Mushrooms and How to Grow Them

1910 1st.edition

Mushrooms, Cucumbers, Salads, Tomatoes

1904 1st.edition
1906 2nd.

Perennials

(1904) 1st.edition
1906 2nd.

Popular Hardy Perennials

1916 1st.edition
(1917) 2nd.
1920 3rd.
(1924) 4th.
1928 5th.

The Book of the Potato

1905 1st.edition
(1911) 2nd.
1917 3rd.

Rock Garden and Alpine Plants

1916 1st.edition
(1917) 2nd.
1922 3rd.
1929 4th.

Root Crops - Potatoes, Onions, Carrots, Turnips

1904 1st.edition
1908 2nd.

Roses

1907 1st.edition

Roses and Their Cultivation

1904 1st.edition
(1905) 2nd.
(1906) 3rd.
(1907) 4th.
1908 5th.
(1909) 6th.
(1910) 7th.
1912 8th.
1913 9th.
1915 10th.
(1917) 11th.
1920 12th.
(1924) 13th.
1931 14th.

Salads and Their Cultivation

1911 1st.edition

Small Gardens

1910	1st.edition
1915	2nd.

Vegetable Foes

1922	1st.edition

Vegetables and Their Cultivation

1905	1st.edition
(1907)	2nd.
(1911)	3rd.
1917	4th.
1919	5th.
1920	6th.
1928	7th.

Window and Indoor Gardening

1911	1st.edition

Window Gardens

1913	1st.edition

BOOKS EDITED BY T.W.SANDERS

( ) = assumed publication date

The Amateur's Flower Garden [Hibberd]
(1898)
1901 revised edition

The Amateur's Greenhouse and Conservatory [Hibberd]
1897

Bees for Profit [Geary]
(1908)

Carnations, Picotees and Pinks [Weguelin]
1900

Chicken Rearing and Incubation [Tysilio Johnson]
(1908)

Chrysanthemums and How to Grow them for Exhibition [Wroe]
1913

Chrysanthemums for Garden and Greenhouse [Crane]
1905 1st.edition
1910 2nd.
1917 3rd.

Cultivated Roses [Piper]
1899

Dairy Cows and the Dairy [Walker]
(1905)

Ducks, Geese, and Turkeys for Profit [Tysilio Johnson]
1904

Easily Grown Hardy Perennials [Vos]
1902

Fowls for Profit [Tysilio Johnson]
1903 (**"Poultry for Profit"**)
1904

Fowls for Profit [Macself]
1917
(1925)

The Goat, Its Use and Management [Bird]
1910 1st.edition
1917 2nd.

Grapes and How to Grow Them [Lansdell]
1907 1st.edition
(1911) 2nd.
1919 3rd.

Green Crops and Herbs for Profit [ed.Sanders]
1903

The Horse, Its Care and Management [Fawcus]
(1905)

Manures for Garden and Farm Crops [Dyke]
1911 1st.edition
1915 2nd.
1924 3rd.
(revised as "**Manures and Fertilizers**")

Orchids for Amateurs [Harrison]
1911

Pansies and Violets [Crane]
1908

Pigs for Profit [Walker]
(1907) 1st.edition
(1908) 2nd.
(1911) 3rd.
1917 4th.

Practical Books on Food Production [ed.Sanders]
1917-8

Rabbits for Profit [Bird]
1904 1st.edition
(1905) 2nd.
(1911) 3rd.
1917 4th.

Rock Gardens and Alpine Plants [Jenkins]
1911

Roots, Bulbs and Tubers for Profit [ed.Sanders]
1903

Rustic Adornments for Homes of Taste [Hibberd]
1895 4th.edition revised

Schools Gardening [Hyde]
1913
1917 ("Simple Gardening")

Sheep, Their Management and Breeding [Muir]
(1910)

The Small Holder's Guide [ed.Sanders]
1910

Tomatoes and How to Grow Them [Castle]
1911 1st.edition
(1912) 2nd.
(1913) 3rd.
1917 4th.
1921 5th.
1925 6th.
1928 7th.
1932 8th.

PUBLICATIONS COMPILED AND EDITED BY T.W.SANDERS

Amateur Gardening
May 1st.1887 - October 23rd.1926

Amateur Gardening Annual and Year Handbook
1912 -1914

Amateur Gardening Popular Handbooks [six parts]
1925-1930 (completed by A.J.Macself)

Profitable Farm and Garden
October 21st.1900 - September 9th.1905

Farm and Garden
September 16th 1905 - February 22nd.1913

The Profitable Farm and Garden Handbooks [fifteen parts]
1903-1910
(also issued as"**Farm and Garden Handbooks**")

Yours Sincerely
T. W. Sanders.